LAWYERS UNDER FIRE

What a Mess Lawyers Have Made of the Law!

BY

AL SAMPSON

First published by AuthorHouse 04/26/04

ISBN: 1-4140-5954-X (e-book)
ISBN: 1-4184-5197-5 (Paperback)
ISBN: 1-4184-5195-9 (Dust Jacket)

Library of Congress Control Number: 2004090941

This book is printed on acid free paper.

Printed in the United States of America
Bloomington, IN

Dedication

To my first wife Irene who would have infuriated the feminists because her greatest goals in life were to be a good wife to me, a good mother to her children, and a good grandmother to her grandchildren, and she surpassed society's highest standards on all three goals. No woman was ever more loved by small children than Irene.

And

To my current wife Mozelle for her moral support

And

To my children, my grandchildren, my friends and their children who will all have to live with the shortcomings of our current legal system unless I and other well intentioned reformers can somehow offer methods to turn the travails of the court system back toward being a total search for the truth

Acknowledgments

I am grateful to the people who have assisted me in the preparation of this book. No such offering can come to life without help from numerous persons, both personal and professional.

First and foremost, I must acknowledge the contribution of my friend, Bill Zarlengo. Bill ignited the spark! At about the time of my 80th birthday, he heard about my earlier book that had been rejected and asked to read the chapters on the practice of law. After doing so, he strongly urged that I end my hiatus and prepare the book that is now Lawyers Under Fire.

Next, I want to thank Judge John L. Kane, Jr, formerly the Senior Judge of the Colorado District of the United States Court of Appeals. The four speeches that Judge Kane delivered at the University of Denver College of Law in 1990 reinforced my beliefs in some of what I planned to write.

Likewise, I wish to express similar gratitude to Deborah Rhode, Director of the Keck Institute of Legal Ethics at Stanford University and to Alan Dershowitz, professor at Harvard University.

I would have liked to have quoted equally from books by Harold J. Rothwax, Jr and Burton S Katz since they discussed issues with such clarity. However, all efforts to reach them both through direct letters and at their publishers were thwarted. Consequently, I severely reduced the number of quotes to well below the limits of fair usage and instead relied on the use of ideas, facts, etc. which are not violations of copyright. Nevertheless, I thank both Judge Rothwax and Judge Katz for providing such excellent sources of information.

Further, I thank a number of doctors and surgeons who granted interviews but who uniformly requested that their name not be put into print because of fear of retaliation from lawyers. Dr. Irl Sell did not survive to see his name, as subject of a prime story, in print.

I also appreciate the proofreading, suggestions, and moral support from Scott Nelson, Phil Sampson, David Sampson, Jeanne Guarneros and Cyndy Sampson.

Finally, I thank John Gilroy for persuading my computer to function at times and in ways that were beyond my knowledge of detailed operation. He helped time after time.

Preface

"A conspiracy of silence shrouds the American justice system. Most insiders – lawyers and judges won't talk. Most outsiders - law professors and journalists - don't really know.

"Some insiders won't talk because they have a stake in not exposing the dark underside of the legal profession. Others are afraid of reprisals."

"…The American justice system is corrupt to the core. It depends on a pervasive dishonesty by its participants. It is unfair…It is discrimination against the poor, the uneducated, the minority groups."

Those written words, encountered after I believed I had entered the final lines of my book, provided an explanation point. Written by Alan Dershowitz, one of the nation's most prominent lawyers and truly prolific legal writers, they amounted to a sweeping condemnation that even I had not been prepared to suggest much as I might have wanted. Yet when I perused those words, I understood that they represented a confirmation of my own feelings that were still in a somewhat formative stage. Maybe some day, I would feel qualified to make such a damning assessment.

The shock of such a firm statement inserted an explanation mark to my lifelong journey to understanding, evaluating and condemning the practice of law. In all of my work on the background study for this book, that single judgment was my greatest surprise. I had understood that there were serious problems, even grievous problems, in the practice of law but never would I have felt sufficiently confident to write words declaring the profession to be totally corrupt.

In early life, I had graduated from Pioneer High School, a small, very rural high school in Oklahoma, so small that we had only eleven students in our graduating class. In what I considered as the basic academic classes of algebra, geometry, geography, history, and English, the education was superb. Yet, there were severe shortcomings. Science was taught from a textbook in which there were two to six chapters for each branch of possibly six sciences. Our library was on two shelves each about 10 feet long. Worst of all, the teaching staff seemed to have made a consistent judgment that the boys would all be farmers. The girls would all become farmer's wives - or teachers. Teaching could be our escape from farming. I think I had assumed at that time that lawyers were people who came from the elite classes or those whom my mother always referred to as "prominent families".

Our class received no orientation on what college could provide or what we could expect. From my own family guidance, I knew that I wanted to "go to college". My mother had briefly been a teacher and my unmarried aunt was still a teacher. Neither of them, however, had explained to me that it would be proper if I were deciding what career field I wanted to pursue. Unbelievable as it may seem, on the night of my graduation from high school, I still did not understand that for college, one must select a field of study. After that ceremony, someone asked me what I would study and I couldn't even provide an intelligent answer.

I enrolled in Cameron University, then a junior college, gradually drifting through three tentative career decisions of mechanical engineering, journalism, and then chemical engineering. One of my enlightenments was that one of my very ordinary friends, Gene Little, was a pre-law student. He certainly would not have qualified to be considered as "elite".

Then came a surprise and unsought appointment to the United States Naval Academy. As a result of political maneuvering, my congressman was in possession of an appointment to the academy and the first requirement was that the name must be submitted by the next day or he forfeited the appointment. That left no time for normal competitive examinations and the congressman had requested a recommendation from the president of the only college in his district.

This was four months after Pearl Harbor and male professors were steadily being called into military or governmental service. Consequently, the college president had formed a committee of three female departmental heads for mathematics, chemistry and physics and they had unanimously recommended me to be recipient of the appointment.

I was called to the president's office and heard the question:

"Are you Alvin Sampson?"

"Yes sir, I am."

"Could you use an appointment to the Naval Academy at Annapolis?"

"I don't know. I've never thought about it." I only knew that I could expect to be drafted shortly and that I wanted a college education.

"Well, the appointment is yours if you want it. But I have to have an answer by tomorrow morning at 10:00 AM"

Thus started my education in matters other than the basic fields of study.

The Naval Academy trains it's future officers in naval law sufficiently that they can serve as recorders, defense attorneys or members of the board for summary courts-martial. The duties of a recorder included serving as prosecuting attorney and legal adviser to members of the court martial panel. Since ships can be at sea for extended periods, especially during war time, the courts-martial were to be conducted without extended delays. Trials would be conducted under prevailing law, Naval Courts and Boards.

I was ordered to serve as recorder one time. The ship to which I was assigned, the U.S.S. Boston, was being deactivated at the Navy Yard in Bremerton, Washington. The crew was to be detached shortly and all officers reassigned as I received my first indoctrination on the improprieties of criminal justice. Commander Hansen, the executive officer, assigned me, as a recent addition to his staff of officers, to be recorder for the trial of a seaman who was charged with theft of government property, specifically a set of mechanic's tools that could be used on his job at a service station offshore.

The first impropriety was that the young man was a member of the division for which I was the division officer. If anything, I should have been the defending officer while some other recently arrived Naval Academy graduate could have served as recorder. When I protested, Commander Hansen, wouldn't hear of the proposed change. I would prosecute James Warren who was present as I tried to ease my way out of the assignment.

Immediately after I returned to my compartment and began to study the information that had been passed to me, Seaman Warren appeared in my room.

"What shall I do, Mr. Sampson? I took the tools but I don't want to get into any more trouble that will hurt my future than I have to. Tell me what I should do." The accused was confessing to the prosecuting attorney.

"First of all, I am going to forget that you said that. You shouldn't be here talking to me because I am going to be forced to prosecute you. You saw me try to get out of it but the Exec wouldn't let me.

"First, you are going to need a defense attorney to give you advice. I understand that Lieutenant Nelson knows more about Naval Law than any officer on the ship."

We went to see Lt. Nelson and he refused the assignment because he feared it would mean that he would be delayed for departure on leave. He would, however, help Warren find some other officer who would serve as defense attorney, and would give advice to the officer who accepted the task.

I returned to my study of the case. I already knew that the charges were questionable but I wanted to review the written law. Then I sought out the witnesses. The principal witness was the commander of the Repair Department who had gone to the service station, confronted Warren and retrieved the tools. He had been accompanied by a petty officer. No one could suggest additional witnesses who had knowledge of the crime, or if potential witnesses knew anything, they wouldn't admit it. There could be no long investigation.

The next morning I went again to the Executive Officer: "Commander, if we are to obtain a conviction against Seaman Warren, the charges should be changed from 'Theft' to 'Unauthorized

Possession of Government Property'. I request that you make that change, sir"

"Why?" he almost roared.

"Because 'Theft' requires that we prove that he personally took the tools off the ship and no one else did. The Repair Officer doesn't know how the tools got ashore and we can't find anyone who does. There will be no problem with the lesser charge of Unauthorized Possession."

Then, the Exec exploded, "There will be no changing the charges. The man is guilty of theft. You had better get a conviction on this case or be ready to resign your commission." (There were two times in my short period in the Navy when I was told to do something that I considered to be improper or be ready to turn in my uniform. That apparently is a standard threat issued by higher officers.)

At that time, all of my ambitions were concentrated on a career in the Navy. That meant that at the trial, James Warren would be charged with 'Theft'.

I presented the best case I could. To "prove" that he had taken the tools ashore, I relied on improper hearsay evidence that one seaman had heard some other seaman say that Warren had taken the tools ashore. I knew that was totally wrong but I had no other evidence.

On a Navy court martial at that time, the recorder sat in the room during deliberations so as to be available to give advice on the law if it was requested by members of the Court Martial board. The board consisted of three officers, all much senior to me, who had been appointed to serve as the equivalent of a jury.

After minimal deliberation, the senior officer summed up the situation.

"We have two choices. There is no way that he should be found guilty of 'Theft'. We can find him innocent and all four of us (the three members of the board and me) will each receive unsatisfactory fitness reports from Commander Hansen. Or, we can find him guilty of 'Theft' and, when the case is reviewed by the Judge Advocate General's office in Washington, we will all receive letters of reprimand for finding Warren guilty without proper proof. But it will probably be several years before that office gets around to reviewing it."

The board opted to avoid the short term, near at hand, wrath of the Executive Officer rather that the distant letter of reprimand from Washington. Seaman Warren received a Bad Conduct Discharge that would severely damage his future applications for civilian work. I later learned that the halls of the Pentagon in Washington were stacked with so many boxes of court martial cases that there was no possibility of all ever being reviewed before everyone had retired unless some Congressman brought pressure on a particular case.

I had received my first exposure to the practice of law even though it was not with lawyers performing in a normal courtroom. I had a taste of both the principles and practices of law, and had learned that the practice of law appealed to me as a life career. Yet, I was uncomfortable with scruples as I saw them in practice, in movies, on the television screen and from the prosecution of Seaman Warren.

From that day forward, two pervading attitudes were evolving within me simultaneously for as long as I would consider career options. First, was the desire to be a lawyer and I knew I was well suited with an ability to reason and an adequate intellectual capacity to compete as a lawyer. In an opposite thrust, however, the second growing self-evaluation, was an unwillingness to abide with what I perceived as the corrupt tendencies of the legal profession.

Instead, I obtained an advanced degree "Business: Industrial Management" from Colorado University and as part of that curriculum obtained top grades in two courses of business law. I credit Professor Joseph L. Frascona with an outstanding, professional job of teaching the theories and intended disciplines of the law. Still, he was teaching arrogance and intimidation along with matters of law.

The first day in class, he said, "You will like this blue text book. It is the best law book ever written. I wrote it."

Later, I was fortunate to attend a one week refresher course on government contract law at George Washington University where I was the only non-lawyer in a class of experienced lawyers.

In my work assignments with three corporations, managers steadily came to credit my legal work on contracts and I basically performed a total of eight years as a contract lawyer.

By the time I reached an age of 45, I had concluded that some day I wanted to write for publication. For the next 30 years, I collected magazine articles and newspapers articles and read books that could provide more background on a wide range of subjects from environmentalism to education to the news media.

Over time, the heaviest concentration of collected material was concerned with improprieties in the practice of law.

In the early 1990s, I prepared a book with an analysis of our educational system, the press, the national deficit, economics, health care, solution to unemployment and a few other subjects. I even had a chapter of advice for Rush Limbaugh. Most importantly, I had 12 chapters on the improper practice of law and corrections that I thought should be made.

Before I even received a rejection from the only agent to whom I submitted it for proposed publication, I had come to understand that the book was too far ranging and the matter of law inadequately researched. The principal comment in that rejection letter was, "Mr. Sampson does not understand the self discipline of lawyers." (My laugh for the day.)

When I made a decision about 8 years later to write this book, I first read over two dozen recent books by lawyers who were critical of existing legal practice. I informed myself on the "self discipline" of lawyers. I also eliminated all subjects from the book except the unfortunate practices of the legal profession and the title became "Lawyers Under Fire."

Still, it was not until I read the sentences by Dershowitz, after all other chapters had been written, that I was prepared to agree with the appraisal that the legal system is "rotten to the core".

Special Note to Readers - I recognize that the word "lawyer "is not a verb and that there is no such acceptable word as "lawyering". Nevertheless, in the context of this book, the term "the non-lawyering public" is such a useful and descriptive phrase to insert instead of the stiff, formal phrases "the members of the public who do not practice law" or "non-members of the legal profession" that I exceed the limits of the English lexicon in order to make a more readable book. I apologize to those purists who are offended by my use of a poorly derived term. I do commonly use the term "lay people" but that seems to me in many instances to be insufficiently inclusive.

Table of Contents

Part I

A Failing Report Card

Part II

True Professionals Recommend Effective Improvements

Part III

Top Goal – An End to the Adversarial System

Part IV

Solutions Needed for Overloaded Systems

Part I

A Failing Report Card

The first sixteen chapters are devoted to educating those lay people who have ignored the need to correct the serious, misguided flaws in the practice of law. How bad can it be? "The profession is rotten to the core."

Chapter 1

"I Hate Lawyers"

Lawyers are today one of our most vexing problems. They are gathering unto themselves an ever-higher portion of the gross domestic product and are assembling a troublesome empire being shaped to be totally under their domination. They have become the "entrenched nobility"!

I could not be more in accord with a phrase that has been used by those who glorify the law; "THE MAJESTY OF THE LAW". How great are the basic premises of law! Although my knowledge and training were insufficient to permit me to join the bar, my studies led me to revere the magnificent logic of the law. The terms are so precisely defined. In proclaimed purpose, at least, truth is the goal. The presiding elders have been given a semblance of respect awarded to men of the clergy or military.

No other field of learning has the splendid logic of the law when undefiled. However, if I revere the law, I have a low opinion of the majority of those who practice the law, and for the practices that obliterate all logical concepts of justice.

Historically, the law has been the noblest of professions, and probably the oldest. Documents describing contracts and litigation have been found that date to about 3000 B.C. That implies a practice of law to some extent. The earliest formal assemblage of the principles of law may have been the Code of Hammurabi, collected in about 1750 B.C., some 400 years before Moses. The earliest presence of lawyers for pay occurred, according to one source, in the Roman era from about 200 B.C. Until then, people were expected to know the laws and customs of society, and participate in litigation personally.

It was not until the twentieth century, maybe even the latter half of that century, that the lawyers began to run tragically amok, and it can be argued that it was the 1976 Supreme Court decision to allow advertising that destroyed the porous walls of disciplined practice. Poll after poll reveals that no class of participants in the American economic system has drawn greater contempt from more people than the lawyers.

We can easily identify the groups who give the lawyers a favorable rating. With those who have little reason to know about lawyers and who have gained their understanding from watching movies and television, the opinion of lawyers is at it's highest. Script writers for "Judging Amy", "The Practice", "Ally McBeal", "Law and Order", "The People's Court", and "The "Prosecutors" have developed a view of the work of lawyers and judges rendering the ultimate of noble conduct. Erle Stanley Gardiner made Perry Mason into one of the world's great fictional heroes. If instead, the people being polled are those who work with lawyers in the business world, on legal proceedings or who come in contact under other circumstances, the poll ratings of lawyers are near the bottom.

Lawyers seemingly believe that the all too frequent phrase, "I hate lawyers" is simply a rhetorical uttering with a faint smattering of truth. But not so! There is a vast reservoir of animosity because of the way that many, maybe most, lawyers have conducted themselves while representing their profession. People resent the greed. They resent the failure to live up to suitable standards of professionalism. They resent the lack of integrity and the arrogance of lawyers And they resent the incivility and lack of attention to the concerns of clients. Several lawyers with whom I have discussed the situation are in full agreement.

The lawyers and the news media like to imply that it is the wealthy financiers who own the large corporations but that isn't the America where every enterprising person has the opportunity to spend

4

less than their total income and invest the rest for a brighter future. The purchase of corporate stock has always been one of the simplest methods of pursuing the American dream. It funds most retirement plans

When the lawyers savagely attack the corporations with their class action lawsuits and punitive awards, they are dimming the prospects for a more affluent future for the Americans with vision. Those lawsuits have seriously impacted the cost of living for every American.

Let's move beyond concern about those persons who express hate for the law and instead, consider what is wrong with the legal profession. Many of the lawyers themselves are deeply concerned by the flaws in the American court system. Books have been written that fault the exclusionary rule, the jury system, the judges, the loss of professionalism, the appellate court system, the supreme court decisions, the high cost of legal work, the inadequacy of pro bono work, the Miranda rule and virtually every aspect of legal practice. And if the problems have been so well identified, solutions or improvements have also been recommended but little ever happens.

Harold J. Rothwax, Jr, former judge on the New York Supreme Court, has presented us with an excellent book entitled, "Guilty: The Collapse of Criminal Justice" in which he warns that:

> "Lawyers simply are not the appropriate persons to correct
> the defects in the adversarial system. Their hearts will never
> be in it, and it is unfair to both their clients and themselves to
> require them to serve two masters."

Yet, the judge didn't mean that changes should be proposed by laymen. He mentions judges but shies away from suggesting that they can do what is needed.

Moreover, the legal justice system and the courts of equity should not be a private domain that is a property of the legal profession. Those systems are the rightful possession of the people of the United States as a whole and should be shaped to serve the needs of society.

Current methods for attempting improvement depend on some single dedicated, high-principled lawyer writing a book with recommended changes in one area and another such lawyer writing a book suggesting changes in a different area. Then other lawyers write articles arguing against the proposed changes. Eventually some board or panel takes action to inject little more than cosmetic changes into the system. In the end, no real benefit is achieved, only that which hurts the fewest possible number of lawyers.

This book will review the damaging actions that are harmful to the practice of law, and present proposed improvements as recommended by dedicated, respected, totally professional members of the bar.

Almost every intelligent attorney who criticizes the existing crisis reports that today's court system is a "lottery." An accused person should be entitled to better than a lottery

Repeatedly, those professionals have written that the non-lawyering public should be involved in the oversight and upgrading of legal practice. Consequently, I will also add a few original ideas of my own that are designed to rectify certain critical faults described by the professionals. So, one member of the public speaks out. The lawyers will be prompt, of course, to declare me to be totally unsuited to offer revolutionary changes to the practices of law

One respected physician from small town America remarked,

> "These people change. I knew some of them when they were kids before they went to law school. They were good kids. Their parents were good people. When they come back from law school, they had changed. They were arrogant. They believe that lawyers are the only ones who know anything."

Indeed, that very philosophy is taught in the law schools.

Paralegals in particular can have a very disapproving view of the men and women who rule their profession.

Today, the number of people who are practicing law in the United States has topped one million and about 38,000 more are being added every year. If the legal profession is the road to power, and if it provides access to wealth and fame, how can we expect it to be otherwise? Today, there are too many lawyers for those who can afford to pay for legal services, and too few for the poor.

With the classroom work that I have described elsewhere, I was able to work as a manager with duties in which I associated with lawyers. I negotiated with and supervised the work of lawyers in the workplace. I corrected the work of lawyers, so, although I had nowhere near the formal training required to be a member of the bar, I did have a fairly extensive knowledge of the practice of law. If not me to speak for the non-lawyering public, who?

At least 100 codes of ethics or civility have been adopted but there are exceptions, exemptions and rules that are not really rules. Deborah Rhode, Professor of Law and Director of the Keck Center on Legal Ethics, has asked us to consider a few of the instructions from one of the codes.

"Lawyers are not to be bullies unless it is 'necessary' or 'proper'...(A lawyer should) be vigorous and zealous on behalf of a client while recognizing, as an officer of the court, that excessive zeal may be detrimental to many clients' interests as well as to the proper functioning of our system of justice...Codes are diplomatically vague...and insufficiently demanding."

The United States is still a democracy, and although threatened by lawyers, the people still rule if we can muster a sufficient majority to demand real change. The battles will have to be fought principally in the state legislatures and in the halls of Congress.

We see two kinds of lawyers in our country. There are honorable, capable, conscientious lawyers functioning within a system that has gone out of control; yet there are a far greater number of reprehensible, unconscionable lawyers functioning within a system that is as bad as the lawyers themselves.

Several writers have reported that 90 per cent of the legal matter that is learned in law school will never be used. And 90% of what will be needed is not taught. Instead, the principal training is to be argumentative, combative, abusive, uncommitted to any given set of beliefs and, unfortunately, arrogant. Author Scott Turow has written that law school drums the humanity out of lawyers.

We could go further and identify those fields of law where impropriety of practice is most extreme and those where the practitioners maintain the highest standards. That temptation would be certain to be an unfair exercise. It is enough to say that some fields of practice are relatively high-principled while others have taken the reputation of the profession into the gutter.

In her book, *The Case Against Lawyers*, Catherine Crier sums up the situation for police on the street,

> "Criminal law now reinforces the notion that cops are better off simply responding to crimes after the fact. Don't take initiative. Don't use common sense and experience. Don't try to stop something before it escalates. Answer those 911 calls, file a report, and wait for the next summons, but remember catch-22. If you don't check or if you fail to follow through when that reasonable officer would have done so, the city and police departments (actually the taxpayers) may be liable for damages in a civil suit."

Someone has to tell it the way it is. Somewhere out there in the millions of pages of legal records, there are a million jumbles of mangled concepts, all pouring forth from some court of justice. Some do not even make sense to a logical mind. Some jumbles contradict other jumbles. Some represent the political agendas of various justices. Some are ambiguous. There are decisions that defy or ignore the provisions of the U.S. Constitution. There are jumbles of mish-mash to represent every illogical concept of rules ever to come to the mind of man.

Then the lawyer must root around among all of those jumbles of incomprehension and sort out the ones that will help him to win the case in process. And if the next day, that lawyer represents a point of opposite principle, there are those jumbled mish-mashes to be found that will serve the other side if the lawyer searches long enough. Or directs some beginning law clerk or paralegal to do the searching. That is the practice of law.

With my training being in engineering and mathematics where precise rules are critical, the many interpretations of legal "rules" and

8

contradictions are beyond me. If I select a very limited concept of law and study that concept as discussed by a half dozen authors, I begin to believe that I understand that one subject. Then I come to a different author who presents an opposite view and the door is wide open again. On appeal, the entire subject can be examined in case after case and eventually total confusion will exist in the matter. Indeed, in law school, lawyers are taught never to be committed to one side of an argument, and the many contradictory stances of the higher courts reflect that fact.

Ultimately, the entire sorry mess can be blamed on all of the decisions made over the years by United States Supreme Courts, the state supreme courts and the various courts of appeal. The myriad decisions have been both inconsistent and politically motivated.

The judgments set forth in the next chapter did not come from this author but rather, from experienced leaders of the profession. Their concerns add up to a complete indictment of the overall profession. If suggested improvements, most recommended by lawyer-critics but some by laymen, could be made to correct the matters of concern, the legal profession could move toward an organization of which every member could be proud

As far as the highest profile field of law, where we seek to improve the criminal justice system, the intent of proposals described in this book is to provide an improved means of arriving at accurate verdicts without significantly violating the constitutional rights of any accused person. The only hope for an improvement of the justice system is that a national consensus must be generated demanding that the legal system shall at least be reformed.

Reform is not enough. A total revolution is needed.

Chapter 2

Opinions from Prominent Members of the Bar

Judge John L. Kane, Jr., former senior judge of the United States District Court of Colorado, provided an appropriate statement when he addressed law students at the University of Denver School of Law:

"The new crisis appears in many guises. There is the public's image of lawyers using the court systems to play games and thwart justice - games such as delays, excessive discovery, excessive fees, contingent fees, crazy lawsuits, public corruption, and financial scandals. There is the profession's dissatisfaction with itself for rudeness, lack of mutual trust, rapacious client stealing and employment practices, which very likely violate the 13th Amendment's proscription of involuntary servitude.

"What is today's crisis? It is frequently expressed by that most inelegant of terms, a loss of professionalism...I regret to say that the courts of this land have been engaged just as much as the lawyers themselves in the unrelenting dismantling of a once proud profession."

A book, to be studied to understand the deterioration of the practice of law, is *The Betrayed Profession* by Sol M Linowitz. Linowitz, now deceased, had a history of fifty years in the practice of law starting as a member of a four-lawyer family practice and continuing through to become a government official in several high level positions, partner of a giant international law firm, and on the way being Ambassador to the Organization of American States under Presidents Lyndon Johnson and Richard M. Nixon, thus earning the title of Ambassador.

Linowitz dealt with the greatness of the past, the decline in service provided in the giant law firms, the reduction in the level of integrity, the pursuit of dollars above all else, the worsening relationships between lawyers and clients, the shallow training of young lawyers in the urban law firms, the desperate need to reassert ethical behavior, the inadequacy of limited legal services to the poor, the decline of the practice of law into the pits as represented by the flood of huckster-shyster TV ads, the failure of lawyers to become well rounded citizens worthy of appointment to positions of honor and power in society, the decline of control of the trials by judges, and symbolically, the decline of the physical condition of courtrooms all over America.

The feeling that lawyers are not trustworthy is the most debilitating aspect of public and client attitudes today.

I must contend that there is no hope for the kind of restoration of professionalism for which Mr. Linowitz pined because water will not run uphill; nor will integrity and morality flow from the debased attitudes of today.

Paul Leonard of the law firm Morrison and Forster has summarized it as follows:

> "We have been paid to be inefficient. It's just kind of grown and grown over generations. The most frightening measure of what the legal profession has lost is that most Americans do not remember the trust that society once placed in lawyers because lawyers are supposed to be the custodian of the community's legal and ethical sense, and if the source of our failure lies in the defects of our education, one of the causes must be our neglect of the law as the subject for study in our schools and colleges. The loss of self respect in the profession and the loss of public respect both reflect the

failure of the schools to convey to the young what the law and lawyers have meant in the history of this country. Not enough is expected of lawyers by the lay public, or within the profession itself, because not enough is known about how lawyers achieved their privileged position...If the profession wishes to retain it's privileges, lawyers above all must understand why they have been granted exclusive access to the judicial processes of government and why the public has a right to expect that they will be vigilant not only in the interests of their clients but also for the rule of the law which protects us all"

The opinion of Judge Rothwax (veteran of the New York Supreme Court) is emphatic:

"The weight of other considerations has made truth subordinate and even irrelevant...The more complex and overburdened our system becomes, the less the truth comes out.

"Day after day, case by case, the results become more ridiculous and more difficult to understand or predict... Committed to the search for truth, the judge is also required by the rules of the game to sit helplessly while skilled professionals are engaged in clear, deliberate and entirely 'proper' efforts to frustrate the search.

"Our courtrooms have become casinos, with a professional culture of misconduct so pervasive and so profound that it is not recognizable as justice."

Joseph Grano, in *Confessions, Truth and the Law* contended,

"The law governing police interrogation in the United States is overly restrictive and formalistic. Commentators frequently assert that the discovery of truth should be the primary or reigning objective of the procedural system. The goal of discovering the truth should have the dominant role in designing the rules that govern criminal procedure.

Frequently, the partisanship of opposing lawyers locks the uncovering of vital evidence or leads to a presentation of vital testimony in a way that distorts it.

"Courts throughout history have succumbed to the temptation to address extraneous issues and sometimes to legislate mini-codes, and Miranda conceivably only carried bad existing judicial practices to new and alarming extremes."

Professor Mirjan Damaska has claimed that the exclusionary rules are much more numerous and surely much more elaborate in America than in any other civilian jurisdiction.

Geoffrey Hazard, professor at Yale, sees the problem as an overall decline of the profession's legitimacy.

"The effect has been no less demoralizing for not being acknowledged. The legal professor no longer enjoys an unchallenged sense of purpose in his traditional practice of mediating through the courts between business enterprise and popular politics. By the same token, the profession no longer presupposes its own identity as the aristocratic element of such a constitutional structure. It's governing norms no longer represent the shared understanding of a substantially cohesive group. They are simply rules of public law regulating a widely pursued technical vocation whose constitutional position is now in doubt...For ordinary people, the worst aspect of a diminished legitimacy of the profession is the danger that the abuse of impositional power by corporate and personal injury lawyers will result in governmental regulation of their use."

Laurence Silberman, former U.S. Deputy Attorney General said,

"The legal process, because of its unbridled growth, has become a cancer which threatens the vitality of our forms of capitalism and democracy."

25 years ago, Yale-trained Anthony Kline, then legal affairs secretary to the governor of California, wrote in the California State Bar Journal,

> "The trial courts are in disarray, mechanisms for the prompt resolution of minor disputes do not exist or are inadequate, the adversary system is in disrepute, the criminal justice system is maligned, legal procedures are in many cases hopelessly arcane and unnecessarily complex, and legal services are becoming prohibitively expensive."

All of those failings have intensified in the years since that was written.

As Chief Justice of the Supreme Court, Warren Burger made the comment that in his time,

> "A lawyer's signature on a pleading of motion was something like a signature on a check. There was supposed to be something to back it up."

Chief Justice Burger estimated that 30% to 50% of all trial lawyers are incompetent. He also said that we may well be on the way to a society overrun by hordes of lawyers, hungry as locusts in numbers never before contemplated.

There was a sharp decline in the respect felt by the public for the Supreme Court throughout the post World War II period. From 83.4% expressing approval in 1949, it went to 32.6% at the end of the anti-establishment revolt in 1973. And by 1993 the approval ratings with the public, according to a Gallup poll, had improved to only 44%. Everyone is conscious of the fact that the judges take home as a reward for their labors perhaps one tenth the financial reward of senior partners in a law firm or a successful personal injury litigator.

Supreme Court Justice Tom Clark labeled bar discipline procedures as a scandalous situation. Few improvements resulted from his declaration and greater transgressions have steadily taken their place.

Although in 1965 and not of recent vintage, Professor Alfred H. Kelly of Wayne State University in Detroit, Mich. wrote,

"Much of the history that the recent Court has produced is of law-office variety. It fails to stand up under the most superficial scrutiny by a scholar possessing some knowledge of American constitutional development.

"The present use of history by the Court is a Marxist-type perversion of the relationship between truth and utility. It assumes that history can be rewritten to serve the interests of libertarian idealism."

(This referred to the Warren Court that issued the Exclusionary Rule and the Miranda Ruling among others.)

Similarly, the following year, Professor Robert G. McCloskey of Harvard University wrote,

"In some notable cases, the Warren Court has with more or less frankness, created constitutional rules out of whole cloth. Whether they are "good" constitutional rules is not here in question. The point is that they were patently judge-made, and modern awareness of this fact may detract from the previous authority that clothed the Court in the past."

Former Los Angeles Judge Burton S. Katz, author of *Justice Overruled,* is greatly concerned about conduct in the courtroom and the lack of adequate resources, both human resources and physical resources. He presents idealistic and practical guidelines of how the trial system could be brought to a level of excellence that the citizens of this nation deserve.

"Too many lawyers are seduced by greed, fame, political ambition, or the fact that the courts have consistently let them get away with misconduct.

"As judges, we see misbehavior so often that we stop being upset…This just breeds contempt for our judges and our judicial system. Trial judges should be on the cutting edge of winning back respect for the bench and our judicial system.

"We are angered at a justice system that mocks the truth, that never seems to fill its promise. We are tired of a system that is more sympathetic to murderers than to victims. The system is broken and needs fixing. The bad news today is that we have done little to fix it. The good news is that we can.

"We must look hard at the adversarial system…Those who think the information brought out of the criminal justice system is the truth, the whole truth and nothing but the truth are fools."

Paul Craig Roberts and Lawrence M. Stratton wrote the following in their book *The Tyranny of Good Intentions*:

"The plight of American democracy is beyond the reach of legal reform alone. Our constitutional system and its precepts have lost the allegiance of American elites."

Debra Rhode, Director of the Keck Center on Legal Ethics at Stanford and past president of the Association of American Law Schools, author of *In the Interests of Justice Reform of the Legal Profession*, and one of the consciences of the legal profession, has provided the following summarizing statements:

"The idealized vision of lawyers as morally independent guardians of justice is out of phase with the prevailing practices…No occupational group, no matter how well intentioned can make unbiased assessments of the public interest on issues that place it's own status and income at risk.

"Much of the problem involves a justice system that is unduly expansive and unresponsive. Ethical rules are undemanding and unenforced. All of these problems have left a growing number of lawyers disaffected and disengaged with their professional lives. Then came the fall, and our own dark ages of crass commercialism, uncivil tactics and amoral advocacy.

"On matters such as excessive fees, unresponsive disciplinary structures, and overbroad protection of the professional monopoly, the public is not ambivalent and its concerns are not unwarranted. The problem is, not so much that the public is uninformed and undecided but that it is unorganized and uninvolved.

"The bar dismisses about 90 percent of complaints about attorneys; less than 2 per cent result in public sanctions. Most litigation misconduct goes unreported and unchallenged. Obstruction, obfuscation, and delay are chronic features of the legal landscape, and money often matters more than merits.

"Discontent within the profession is considerable. The focus is on power and money, winners and losers, movers and shakers, but, at intervals, worries about the loss of professional souls. A majority of lawyers report that they would choose another career if they had it to do over again. Three fourths do not want their children to be lawyers. Only one fifth feel like the profession has lived up to their expectations in contributing to the social good. An estimated one third of American attorneys suffer from depression, or alcoholism or drug addiction. That is two or three times higher than the public generally."

Rhode is not totally negative in her assessment of the legal profession as she denies certain claims made by politicians. She points out that lawyers are the custodian of American political, social, economic institutions, and their regulation should be a matter of broad social concern. The legal profession is also responsible for much that is the best in democratic processes. Lawyers have been architects of the governmental structure, the model for much of the world. They have been leaders in virtually all movements of social justice in the nation's history.

In a New York Times article titled, "Why Lawyers Lie", lawyer Floyd Abrams wrote,

"It is time to ask whether it really leads to justice to have a system in which lawyers spend far more time avoiding truth than finding it."

Professor John Langbein of Yale Law School has summed up his impression of the profession:

"The truth is, we have a legal system that is a laughing stock in the civilized world. We have a legal system that encourages people not to want to do business with this country. We have a legal system that is ever more expensive, that causes us to pay monumental insurance premiums by comparison with the rest of the civilized world. We have a legal system that is a flop."

The paragraphs of Alan Dershowitz that were used to begin the preface are worth repeating since too many readers will have by-passed that opening estimate of the legal situation. They are the initial lines of the introduction to his book *"The Best Defense"*:

"A conspiracy of silence shrouds the American justice system. Most insiders – lawyers and judges –won't talk. Most outsiders – professors and judges – don't really know. Few of those outside the club ever get close enough to the day to day operation of the system to appreciate how it really works.

"Some insiders won't talk because they have a stake in not exposing the dark underside of the legal profession. Others are in fear of reprisals. Indeed, the formal rules governing the legal profession discourage lawyers from criticizing their 'professional brethren,' and encourage them to promote 'public confidence' in our courts and in the 'honor of our profession'...Equally important is the understanding among insiders that they should criticize the system only within the club and not in public. The dichotomy between insiders who know but won't say and outsiders who will say but don't know has deprived the public of a realistic assessment of the American justice system.

"The American justice system is corrupt to the core: It depends on a pervasive dishonesty by its participants. It is unfair: it is discrimination against the poor, the uneducated, the minority groups..."

From Russia came a more philosophical bent. Alexander Solzhenitzen declared in an address to Harvard University in 1979:

"I have spent all my life under a Communist regime and I will tell you that a society without any objective legal scale is a terrible one indeed. But a society with no other scale than a legal one is also less than worthy of men. A society based on the letter of the law and never reaching any higher, fails to take advantage of the full range of human possibilities. The letter of the law is too cold and formal to have a beneficial influence on society. Whenever the tissue of life is woven of legalistic relationships, this creates an atmosphere of spiritual mediocrity that paralyzes man's noblest impulses."

Other critics abound within the profession.

Some of these authorities, Kane, Rothwax, Grano, Katz, and Rhode will be quoted extensively in the second section of this book where I present the recommendations for improvement as developed within the legal profession.

Chapter 3

Issues of Mangled Professionalism

In order to present a list of shortfalls to professionalism as lawyers would state them, we turn chiefly to a book by the lawyer who is the Director of the Keck Center of Legal Ethics at Stanford University. In her book, *"In the Interests of Justice - Reforming the System of Justice"*, Deborah Rhode discusses every aspect of the problems. Many of her criticisms are duplicated by other writers but her written comments can be used to introduce the non-lawyer to the yawning chasm of conflicts with professionalism that need to be overcome.

Justice John L. Kane added some specific problems to the list. Many flaws have been named repeatedly by one author after another.

So what are the detailed shortcomings that have been pinpointed by esteemed members of the legal profession - by those who have written books on the subject?

A. Codes of Conduct
1. Codes of conduct need to be written which have substantial meaning. There are at least 100 codes of conduct that have been issued but they are written in vague terms so that they are insufficiently demanding and inadequately enforced. (Rhode)
2. Few lawyers would support an ethical rule that expressly authorized advocates to "do everything the law allows to

20

disconcert, distress, divert, disturb, deflect, deceive, disorder, delude, dupe and distract their opponents". But in practice, many lawyers have supported adversarial norms that permit exactly that. (Rhode)
3. The bar dismisses about 90 percent of complaints about lawyers. In fact, in one sampling of 380 cases of serious misconduct, not a single one resulted in disciplinary actions. (Rhode)
4. Obstructionism is a chronic feature of legal conduct. (Kane).
5. Most litigation misconduct goes unreported and unchallenged. (Numerous lawyers)
6. Less than 2 per cent of complaints result in public sanctions. (Rhode) (The author had a sound cause for charging an attorney with a violation of ethics as described in Chapter 15, but was urged by a representative of the state bar headquarters to do nothing.)

B. Greed
1. Excessive fees are widespread and may even be universally out of line. (Numerous lawyers)
2. When financial scandals erupt, lawyers are almost always involved in creating the structure which caused the scandal. (Kane)
3. Neither market nor regulatory structures alone can fill the gap or cope with all of the opportunities for lawyers to favor their own interests over those of the public. (Rhode)
4. Several nations prohibit contingency fees because they are considered to be a source of evil. (Numerous lawyers)

C. Failed Attempts at Reform
1. Although innumerable bar conferences, commissions and committees have been established, they have failed to produce the reform necessary to achieve improvement. (Rhode)
2. Control over legal processes and legal ethics have been left to the organized bar, the very group least capable of disinterested decision making. (Rhode)

3. Those who are committed to reform have been hobbled by the bar's own political and economic interests which push in the opposite direction. (Rhode)
4. In jurisdictions that fail to provide the necessary financial support for appointed counsel, courts need to find constitutional violations and to develop appropriate remedies. (Rhode)

D. Public Involvement

1. The independence of the profession from governmental domination deserves protection but not at the cost of preempting public accountability (Rhode)
2. Although lawyer conceived regulatory codes claim to protect the public, the public has almost no voice in their content or reinforcement. The public should be given a greater voice in over-sight structures. The legal system lacks public accountability. Ordinary citizens are locked out of the regulatory decisions that affect the justice system. Public interests should play a more central role in the regulatory process under which lawyers operate. (Rhode)
3. Consumer regulation experts, public interest organizations and competing occupations should accept the requirement that they have representation in the process of regulating lawyers. (Rhode)
4. Professional conduct implicates public values and representatives of the public should figure most prominently in the formulation and enforcement of professional standards. (Rhode)
5. The public and the profession need to work together on reforms to reconnect the ideals and institutions of legal practice. (Rhode)
6. Regulation of the legal profession has been designed by and for the profession, and too often protects its concerns at the public's expense. (Rhode)
7. For minor grievances involving neglect, delay and overcharging, the bar should develop alternative dispute

resolution systems that satisfy the public, not the profession. (Rhode)

E. Forbidden Behavior
1. Client stealing should be eliminated. (Kane)
2. Experts are too often presented as witnesses who are not truly experts in the declared field of expertise to which they testify. (Numerous Lawyers)
3. Restrictions should be placed on games that lawyers play. (Kane)
4. When public corruption occurs, lawyers can almost always be found to be involved. (Kane)
5. Too many crazy lawsuits have been initiated by lawyers. (Kane)
6. Curbing adversarial excesses will require more effective prohibitions on delay, distortion, and deception. (Numerous lawyers)

F. Discipline
1. At a minimum, lawyers complaint records should be open to the public, and disciplinary agencies should have expanded resources, jurisdiction and remedial options. (Rhode)

G. Improper Allocation
1. The current system offers overly zealous representation for those can afford it. (Numerous lawyers).
2. The current system offers inadequate representation for everyone except those with a large amount of money. (Numerous lawyers)
3. The public deserves access to legal assistance and to legal process that satisfies standards of fairness, integrity, and efficiency. (Rhode)

H. Competition
1. The appropriate response to market values is to harness and learn from competition, not to suppress it. (Rhode)
2. Lawyers have blocked efforts to simplify services and increase access to non-lawyer providers. (Rhode).

I. Alternative Processes

1. Graduates of the limited degree programs, along with other qualified non-lawyers, should be permitted to offer routine services, subject to ethical requirements regarding competence, conflicts of interest, confidentiality, malpractice insurance, and so forth. (Rhode)
2. The public should have more opportunities for alternative dispute resolution procedures and more information about the effectiveness of those alternatives. (Numerous lawyers)
3. Clients choosing lawyers, lawyers choosing dispute resolution processes, attorneys choosing law firms, and students choosing law schools all should have more options and more reliable information about the options available. (Rhode)
4. Rules concerning "unauthorized practice" by out of state lawyers and non-lawyer competitors should reflect client interests in cost-effective services, not local practitioner's interests in preserving their monopoly. (Rhode)
5. Non-lawyer specialists and multidisciplinary collaborations should be regulated rather than repressed, and their regulatory framework should be designed by more disinterested decision makers than the organized bar. (Rhode).

J. Law Schools

1. Law school accreditation requirements and ranking systems could do more to hold educators accountable for their performance along dimensions such as diversity, professional responsibility instruction, pro bono programs, skills training, and interdisciplinary opportunities. (Rhode)
2. Law schools should offer a broader range of degree programs including shorter training for limited practices. (Rhode)
3. Decisions about admission, discipline, competition, confidentiality and malpractice should be given more

involvement by judges, legislatures, administrative agencies, and consumer organizations. (Rhode)
4. The present ethics curriculum is inadequate. Opportunities for systemic reflection during practice is too rare. (Rhode)
5. Specialized educational programs should focus more attention on the cost, regulation, and distribution of legal services. (Rhode)

K. Civil Law
1. Methods should be identified to minimize excessive discovery. (Kane)

L. Life's Rewards for Lawyers
1. Bar efforts have failed to respond to lawyers' own dissatisfaction with their professional lives. (Rhode)
2. The priority of profits and resulting sweatshop schedules have squeezed out time for public service and family commitments. (Rhode).
3. The greatest source of discontent among today's lawyers is their perceived lack of contribution to social justice (Numerous)
4. Equal opportunity remains an aspiration without any real commitment. Race and gender bias are condemned in principle but commonly overlooked in practice. (Numerous)
5. No occupation offers greater opportunity in power, money, and status but lawyers pay the price in disproportionate rates of stress, depression and substance abuse. (Rhode)
6. Many lawyers have lost connection with the ideals of social justice that led them into law originally. (Numerous)
7. Socially responsible behavior by lawyers should be rewarded to encourage individuals to select practitioners with strong ethical reputations. (Rhode)

M. Appropriate Approved Standards
1. Categorical prohibitions on undignified marketing and direct client contact should be replaced with more targeted regulations aimed at fraud, exploitation, and invasions of privacy. (Rhode)

2. More effort should be made to identify and deter misconduct through strategies such as random financial audits, free assistance with complaints and enforcement of rules requiring lawyers to report serious ethical violations. A wider range of sanctions and a greater willingness to impose them are critical. (Rhode)
3. The priority of profits and resulting sweatshop schedules have squeezed out time for public service and family commitments. (Rhode)
4. Standards could require procedures concerning ethical training, supervision, pro bono service and related concerns (Rhode)
5. Concentrate on developing mutual trust. (Rhode)
6. Rudeness should be replaced by high standards of decorum in interpersonal contacts. (Rhode)
7. Socially responsible behavior should be rewarded to encourage individuals to select practitioners with strong ethical reputations. (Rhode)
8. As officers of justice, lawyers should assume greater obligations to pursue justice. (Rhode)
9. Lawyers should provide clients with a "bill of rights" about their representation, better access to their legal rights and their lawyer's performance. (Rhode)
10. Commercialism and incivility are increasing while collegiality and collective responsibility are in decline. (Rhode)
11. Regulations concerning advertising, solicitation, and non-lawyer practice need to focus more on protecting the public and less on protecting the profession. (Rhode)
12. Lawyers should adhere to suitable proportions of pro bono work. (Rhode)
13. Lawyers need to assume greater moral responsibility for the consequences of their professional conduct and for the adequacy of their own regulatory processes and working conditions (Rhode)

14. Lawyers should provide their clients with information about the disciplinary process and the ethical records of individual lawyers. (Rhode)
15. Lawyers should have obligations to disclose material evidence and confidential information necessary to prevent significant professional or physical injury. (Rhode)

What a superb list of standards! If the legal profession would adopt and practice the improvements listed in paragraph M, it would be a near ideal situation for our society, our nation, and for every citizen of the United States!

Chapter 4

The Monstrous Gap in Legal Service

With great self-soothing claims about pro bono work, lawyers leave a major portion of the population, maybe one third, without effective legal service of any kind. The major law firms are located in the large cities and in a bid to provide themselves with a good public relations front, provide some measure of pro bono work to the inner city poor. Critics pronounce that the amount is far less than that stipulated in the codes of ethics but at least there is a measure of legal assistance.

But what of the great number of people who, often clustered in small towns of America, simply do without legal help because it is unavailable?

Add to that the number of working poor whose income is barely sufficient to provide their own minimum standard of living. Many of these persons do not even know what pro bono work is. Small town lawyers are not prone to contribute pro bono work and the residents simply do without. I think it is a fair estimate that the segment of population unable to pay for legal work ranges up to the 45th percentile level of income.

Whenever any attorney makes an effort to discuss standards of professional conduct, the inevitable response is to mention pro bono work. Unfortunately, in the crush of business, the pro bono work is the first thing to be omitted from the schedule.

If there has been a survey to identify the segment of the poor who are the recipients of pro bono work that is performed, it has escaped my attention. Cant we image that it is the poorest of the welfare ranks of the inner city who are primarily targeted for pro bono assistance? That may be as it should be, but what of the great multitude of Americans whose level of earnings fall just above the welfare ranks and whose top level is such that every dollar has to be stretched to provide for more mundane necessities. Do they receive pro bono assistance? I don't think so. Can they afford to pay for legal help at today's fee schedules? They cannot. Maybe my percentiles are skewed from reality but I contend that there is a great mass of people who need legal assistance, can't afford it and don't get it.

I inquire of the professionals if the pro bono work is filling this demand. If a member of this segment needs a will, they do without. If they enter into an agreement where they should have a simple contract, they do without.

Let me describe a case where the subject should have had pro bono help. A man, whom we will call Monte, and his wife had a small income that came from his wife's tiny Social Security check and his own Social Security Supplemental Insurance, the assistance that is available to handicapped citizens above age 60. Monte had suffered minor brain injury and he and his wife lived in a rented mobile home.

Monte first told me how fortunate he was that he had encountered an elderly man, "Bob", who owned the remnants of a mobile home where everything had been stripped down to the floor. Bob had offered that if Monte would help him with the labor to rebuild the mobile home, the unit would belong to Monte. (I later extracted the fact that what Bob meant was that Monte's labor would serve as a down payment but Monte didn't understand that distinction.) Bob could provide most of the materials and Monte would make a small contribution.

The two men (and Monte's wife) went to work and toiled for 11 months. Monte was extremely proud that he was building a home that would one day be his own. He periodically sent me pictures of himself and his wife at work.

Then Percy, the more knowledgeable son of Bob's separated wife, got into the act and proclaimed that the planned total sale price was too low. (Actually, it was unreasonably high.) He was going to block the deal. I asked Monte if he had a written contract and, of course, there was none. He searched for a lawyer who would help and could find none who would accept his case unless he paid a retainer. Naturally, Monte had no money for a retainer. No lawyer was offering pro bono work in that small town. Bob's wife came and went and when she was out of town, the problem temporarily disappeared.

After asking Monte if Bob would now sign a contract, I questioned him at length to determine the true intent of the verbal agreement. I then prepared a one page contract to cover the situation. Monte, however, could never quite get the courage to pressure Bob into signing the contract. Bob always verbally assured him that the original deal was going to be good and "Bob is a good guy".

The two men completed the mobile home to the best of their diminished abilities, with corners that weren't square and floors that sloped in some areas. Monte and his wife moved in and were proud of their new home.

Then the wife returned from out of state and, with her son's help, filed for divorce. Since the son was able to afford an attorney, a divorce settlement was reached in which the wife was awarded the mobile home. She immediately served an eviction notice to Bob and his wife. The final result was that Monte received not one penny of pay for 13 months of daily labor or for materials that he had supplied. His wife had worked less so she lost less.

That is an actual, true prototype of the class of people who need pro bono work and don't get it. Project that example into the millions and we have an enormous class of neglected poor.

I have one other question to ask the lawyers. I read about the legal clinics that sometimes occur in the heart of urban problem areas. Some lawyers do heroic work in behalf of that clientele. But what of the rural poor, the great mass of people who encounter problem circumstances where someone is violating their rightful situation? Or how about the residents of very small towns? Monte had never heard of pro bono work. Probably, none of his neighbors had either. The term 'Pro bono work' was meaningless. Does some well meaning lawyer ever hold a meeting to orient these ne'er-do-wells? And even if they had heard of it, then no pro bono assistance is available. Lawyers gravitate to the larger cities.

Chapter 5

A Distorted Definition of Truth

No non-lawyer can begin to understand the detachment that the lawyers have for the goals that we would set for them until we comprehend the differing definitions that we and they have for the word "truth". That word simply does not mean the same to lawyers as it does to most Americans.

For the reader who would learn more about the definition of truth as only being determined with juries composed of a fair representation of all biases, the book, *"We, the Jury"* by Jeffrey Abramson, provides a full explanation. For the lawyer, truth is a trial decision democratically reached by due process of law before a jury that represents a proportionate share of all biases of the community.

A simple illustration will clarify how researchers can reach two very different versions of truth. I am sure that, in the decades before the civil rights struggle of the 1960s, there were sincere, well intentioned, scholarly individuals or groups in the South who set out to answer the question of whether or not the Blacks had sufficient natural intelligence to accomplish high school and college work. They selected sample groups to be studied, developed methods of measuring capabilities, and analyzed their results with care. Unfortunately, their personal biases affected the outcome and the final judgment was that the Black students simply were not born with an equal intellect with white persons.

With rare exceptions, they concluded, the average Black would be better served by limiting his study to possibly the eighth grade. The scholars published their papers to explain their results. The "truth" had been determined.

In a different atmosphere where the same biases were absent, meanwhile, there were similar scholars who crafted their own study methods to answer the same questions. They selected their samples, shaped their methods of research and studied their data. They may have been 100% logical or they may have incorporated some of their own biases. The faulty results of the segregationists' study had not taken into consideration the difference made by pre-conditioning. Small white children had sat on their grandmother's lap while books were read to them. They had grown to school age in a home atmosphere where learning was revered and it was expected that they would learn.

In comparison, the Blacks had grown to school age without being introduced to books. The teachers in the early years of school were overloaded and inadequately trained. Decades later, schools would address that problem by providing programs called "Head Start" and "Follow Through".

Voila! The "truth" had been found. For the integrationists, Blacks, with proper advanced conditioning, were capable of performing equal academic work.

Both groups achieved a version of what the authors considered to be truth. In the South, the decision was that Blacks were born with an inability to do high school work while in the north the results showed that they were capable of doing the same work as White children.

Non-lawyers almost unanimously cling to a definition of "truth" as meaning the actual facts as they happened or as they exist. For the lawyers, the key determination is not what actually happened but truth according to the method by which the "truth" was achieved.

Over centuries of practice, lawyers have achieved hundreds of rules that are seen as protecting the constitutional rights of the accused. The most dominating rule of that nature is the exclusionary rule that most lawyers consider to be sacrosanct but which very sincere, scholarly lawyers consider to be a cancer in the system. Similarly, the Miranda rule helps to shape the truth. Or does it?

Initially, Blacks had been excluded from juries and after the civil war the northern states began to include them. Still the southern states persisted with all white juries. The government steadily moved to correct perceived injustices until it was ruled that all juries must include a number of blacks roughly proportional to the number of blacks in the applicable community.

In 1920, the constitution was amended to give women the right to vote and that immediately brought demands that they also be allowed to serve on juries. That led to disputes as to what proportions of women, and more particularly, whether there were certain crimes that demanded a higher proportion of females. Many thought that most of the jurors on a rape trial should be women because they could empathize with the victim. Others contended that a higher proportion of males would protect the rights of the accused.

The courts became dissatisfied with basing jury makeup on random selection from the voter rolls because they are not a fair cross section of the population. Blacks, Hispanics, the young and the poor do not register to vote in equal numbers to the rest of the population. Consequently, the juries were not including a fair share of biases. In most states, the voter registration lists have been abandoned in favor of driver's license lists.

The perfect example to illustrate the different result to be reached within a court of law was the Clinton-Lewinsky relationship that dominated the nation's attention during the final years of President Bill Clinton's term. Lawyers from the White House repeatedly stated that the truth had not been established and as long as that was true, they would consider the president to be innocent. They knew they were safe because under their standards truth had never been legally established until the matter had been adjudicated. If Clinton were to be tried in a court of justice, they were confident that he would be tried before a mostly Black jury from Washington, D.C. a jury whose voting patterns would be heavily Democratic. Blacks have always been heavily partial to Clinton. In front of any such jury, he would surely have been found not guilty. Therefore, they could declare again and again that the truth would show him to be innocent. Hilary stated firmly in one press conference that the truth had not been established.

To develop representative participation in juries, the court system is rejecting the normal definition of truth upon which we, the lay people, have relied for over a thousand years. Truth, according to the courts, is a sampling of truth shaped by the evidence but redefined according to the weighted impacts of all prejudices in the community. Prejudices trump old-fashioned truth.

It is interesting to note that the law dictionary that I use contains over 5000 legal terms but does not provide a definition of truth. The definition that I would have expected to find would have been similar to the following: "Truth is constituted by a version of facts based on a jury decision reached by due process of law with a jury composition matching proportional population groups in the community."

So much for a tentative description of the lawyer's version of truth. Why couldn't the author of the dictionary have revealed one of the secrets of the legal profession?

Chapter 6

Morality and the Law

The foundation of today's legal practice consists of the shifting sands of morality. Most Americans support morality but need to be enlightened about the lawyer's view.

A brief quiz follows: True False

1. The ultimate basis of all legal proceedings in courts of the United States is the U.S. Constitution that was adopted in 1787 and the amendments that have been added to it.   ____ ____

2. Law is rooted in a clear foundation of moral principle.   ____ ____

3. The only way in which the impact of the constitution can be changed is through the amendment process.   ____ ____

When the constitution was first adopted in 1787, most of the founding fathers supported the affirmative answers but elitists of the legal profession would change the very basic concepts of the constitution - without amendment. All of the above statements must now be declared to be false.

Sanford Levinson, a teacher of Politics at Princeton University, presented an article in Harper's Magazine, for which the very title says a great deal about the lawyer's view of morality

That article was headed, "The Specious Morality of the Law", specious meaning "seemingly fair, attractive, sound or true, but not actually so. Deceptive" Or in another definition, "Having a false look of genuineness"...or "having a deceptive attraction".

Levinson wrote:

"(John) Adams' notion of the rule of law was based on this older conception of the law as rooted in a common religious and moral order. Adams viewed individuals as members of political communities to which they would be willing to subordinate their selfish personal interest in behalf of a 'common good'. For Adams and the older generation, law was based on moral principle."

Langdell Hall at the Harvard Law School features the statement of medieval jurist Henry de Bracton "Not Under Man, But Under God and the Law.".

Some of our most prominent presidents violated the constitution. Two of those violations were clearly in the best interest of our country, a third may have been questionable but prudent and the final one a horrible violation of the rights of citizens, even though the violation was performed with the best of intentions.

Thomas Jefferson is generally considered to be the first president to significantly deviate from the exact content of the constitution. Opposing senators argued that no provision existed that would have permitted Jefferson to authorize the Louisiana Purchase. Since it added the territory that would become part or all of 15 states, no one today would object that Jefferson was exceeding the powers granted to the president under the constitution. Yet, that act established the precedent that the president could ignore the constitution when expedient and for the best interest of the young nation.

Most scholars would consider that the most serious infractions ever perpetrated against the constitution were two actions by Abraham Lincoln. Worst of all was the suspension of the writ of Habeas Corpus during the Civil War. Lincoln had previously asserted that "Every American must swear...never to violate in the least particular, the laws of the country, and never to tolerate violations by others."

The provision in the constitution was that: "The privilege of the writ of Habeas Corpus shall not be suspended, unless when cases of rebellion or invasion of the public safety may require it." The Civil War did not comply with the definition of rebellion since that must be an organized opposition intended to change or overthrow the existing government or ruling authority.

Lincoln's second major violation of the constitution was the Emancipation Proclamation which freed the slaves. That act was promptly reinforced by amendments to the constitution so that no one then or now seriously criticizes him for that step. Maybe unanimously, the citizenry agree that it was a proper action that prevented delays that would have been required for the proper ratification process.

Franklin Roosevelt also seriously violated the constitution when he ordered residents of Japanese origin to be interned during World War II

While these ventures provided precedents for overstepping the strict intentions of the Constitution, the truly sweeping movements would wait the terms and writings of Chief Justice Oliver Wendell Holmes Jr.

His father, Oliver Wendell Holmes, the son of a strict Congregationalist minister had, as a teenager, rebelled in a fashion to be a role model for the "hippies" of the 1960's. Not a serious scholar until he took an interest in medicine, Holmes had been fighting against the beliefs of his parents who would have spread liberal religious ideas.

Unwilling to accept the dogmas presented to him at Harvard, the decisions by the son, Justice Oliver Wendell Holmes, Jr, on the

Supreme Court of the United States, would reflect the leanings of his father's opposition to any current version of morality.

In 1903, after twenty years of service on the Supreme Courts of New York and the United States, Holmes wrote,

"While the courts must exercise judgments of their own, it is by no means true that every law is void which is…based upon a conception of morality with which they disagree. Considerable latitude must be allowed for differences of view…Otherwise, a constitution, instead of embodying only relatively fundamental rules of right, as generally understood by all English speaking communities, would become the partisan set of ethical or economical opinions, which by no means are held by all."

Thus began the trip down the slippery slope to the elimination of morality from the law. The issue of morality had encountered the unstoppable slide.

A general pattern of thought soon developed which considered that moral foundations of the constitution were not truly relevant. Mr. Holmes, with his disciple, Justice Felix Frankfurter, annunciated into law the principle that morality was to be ignored.

Quoting Levinson in regard to the words of Holmes:

"No longer need law be based on moral principle; instead it receives its legitimacy from incarnating the focused energies by the body politic…Any guarantee that fidelity to law necessarily will mean equal fidelity to principles of moral conduct vanishes…

"Law is stripped of moral anchoring, becoming instead the product of specific political institutions enjoying power under the Constitution.

"Holmes regarded the problem of coming to terms with the existence of moral evil in the world as 'drool', and he had only contempt for those who took the problem seriously. Both (Holmes and Frankfurter) defined the task of courts in a democracy as giving almost unrestrained enforcement to popular will as measured by the legislative process."

The concept that morality is no longer to be a viable part of our constitution stems from the viewpoint that one person's notion of morality may be quite different from that of another. It would follow, then, that one person's concept of morality should not be forced on another. The law, therefore, prefers no inclusion of morality in interpretations rendered by judicial authorities.

The refusal to accept a rather rigorous view of what is moral and what is immoral ignores the history through which fairly consistent concepts of morality have been handed down from generation to generation from Judaic times.

A final statement from Mr. Levinson,

"The constitution of 1787 is related to today's constitution only in metaphysical ways."

Can it be a coincidence that the period during which morality was being expurgated from law coincided with the period in our history when the rate of crime in the United States has been spiraling? That has not been happenstance…Instead, it is now perfectly acceptable to introduce filth into the classroom. Every kind of anti-American demagoguery is considered proper and educational. Educators are promoting introduction of sexual material into the classroom at the earliest possible age, even at the level of kindergarten, under the guise of sexual education. Everything is being promoted for the education of children except God, the foundation of the faith of our fathers.

In a search for writings on the relationship between morality and law, I discovered the work of Lon L. Fuller, a professor who had taught at Oregon, Illinois, Duke and Harvard. According to Professor Fuller, the methods by which a law can fail to pass tests for adequate morality, i.e., the eight distinct routes to immorality are (1) a failure to achieve any rules, (2) a failure to publicize, (3) the abuse of being retroactive, (4) a failure to make rules understandable, (5) the enactment of contradictory rules (6) rules that require conduct beyond the power of the affected party, (7) introducing such frequent changes in the rules that the subject cannot orient to the new rules and (8) a failure of congruence between the rules as announced and their actual administration. Rules, rules, rules.

Another episode illustrates the depth to which the "entrenched nobility" has descended. In 1988, our Littleton United Methodist Church chose to conduct a discussion series on ethical conduct in the world of business. In preparing for this series, Doctor Richard Evans, the associate pastor, and I consulted with members of the legal faculty at Denver University to scope content for the sessions. Dr Evans concluded that it would be desirable to invite one of those law professors to lead our group as an introductory orientation to the subject. He invited one of the lawyers who served as instructor of ethics in the legal department at the university to provide a basis for group interaction.

That faculty member declined to participate. He stated that he was afraid that he could possibly be sued because of some statement that he might make about ethics. Specifically, he said, some member of the discussion group might act in accordance with something that he portrayed as ethical, and some opposing attorney might choose to claim that statement constituted malpractice of law. He would be vulnerable to a lawsuit.

To this our society has fallen, to the level where a prominent lawyer, a member of the faculty of an eminent university, is afraid to express an opinion on what constitutes proper ethics. If we cannot decide on what is ethical and moral, we certainly cannot correct the abundance of criminal activity in our nation. Are ethics so far outside the lore of lawyers that they cannot even discuss the subject? Cannot we as a society even discuss the subject?

To summarize what has been described above, the Constitution of the United States now has stature only as a tool for the lawyers. When it serves their purpose in legal procedures currently underway, they can hail and venerate the constitution as a sacred part of our heritage. But when it serves the purposes of the lawyers to ignore that famous document, reasoning can be developed by which the paper can be regarded merely as a cherished relic of the past.

It has all occurred by a process of gradualism. Generally, each decision moves the process a little farther than the previous one. And over two centuries of changes and one or two major steps that went essentially unnoticed, our constitution has been altered for selective usage.

■ ▪ ■ ▪ ■ ▪ ■ ▪ ■ ▪ ■ ▪ ■ ▪ ■ ▪ ■ ▪ ■ ▪ ■ ▪ ■

Before we leave the subject of ethics and morality, we must present the three unexpected questions as posed by Professor Monroe Friedman, a leading ethics scholar - unexpected because the answers seem so obvious - and the three vile answers - vile because they frame the basic ethos for innumerable defense attorneys of America.

In 1966, Professor Monroe, specialist on ethics, asked what he described as the "Three Hardest Questions" (of a defense attorney)

1. Is it proper to cross-examine for the purpose of discrediting the reliability or credibility of an adverse witness whom you know to be telling the truth?
2. Is it proper to put a witness (including the defendant) on the stand when you know he will commit perjury?
3. Is it proper to give your client legal advice when you have reason to believe that the knowledge you give him will tempt him to commit perjury?

Professor Friedman answered all of these questions in the affirmative – and thus launched a storm of controversy that is yet to settle. The new "Procedures for Court Room Practice" adopted in 1986 attempted to overrule those guidelines but for numerous attorneys, these responses still lie at the heart of their moral stance. They are everyday practices.

Thus, we have seen how the legal profession, particularly the jurists and the writers, made an assault upon morality to their own benefit.

Chapter 7

The Nature of Civil Law

While we have declared the purpose of this book to be to educate the lay public, the abundance of criminal cases on television and in the motion pictures has already provided a reasonable familiarity with the rules and procedures of criminal law. That is not true with civil law as its characteristics are basically the law of the wealthy.

The second O.J. Simpson case was a highly publicized civil case and had all of the same ingredients as any other civil case: endless legal maneuvering, discovery, motion practice, the struggle to uncover every last bit of information, building your own case to the last, minute detail, and presenting the arguments and evidences to the judge and jury to persuade them that your side is right and the other side is wrong. Simpson was found guilty of murder but that was for the purposes of awarding monetary compensation and was nothing for which he could be punished in his person.

Civil law covers corporate law, tax law, litigious law, securities and bond issues, antitrust law, water law and the like. For these, there is much less comprehension among the public. Yet, there are many flaws and improper practices that need to be corrected.

Since the upcoming chapters deal chiefly with civil suits, we can create a better understanding by presenting concepts that are basic to civil law.

The purposes of the two types of law are different. In criminal law, the issue is to convict some person or group of persons of criminal activity and to punish the person who has been found guilty. In civil law, the purpose is usually to cause money to be transferred from one wealthy person to another wealthy person. A punishment in a civil case can in no way effect the person of the defendant – no death penalties, jail sentences, or probations.

In civil law, no one is concerned about a speedy trial. Instead, the preparation can last many months or even years. Some appeals continue for decades. The participants often do not, in fact, want to go to a jury trial because they do not want to trust their fortunes to the whims of a jury that lacks understanding of the complex issues and that is stocked with biases favorable to the other side. Instead, clients hire lawyers to place them in the best possible position. They make every effort to assure that their clients are in a status so that an understanding can be reached that will result in an agreement without going to trial.

Still, there is the litigious law where the purpose of the lawyer for the plaintiffs is to convince a jury of minimum intelligence that enormous judgments should be made against the defendants.

In criminal law, the preparation consists of developing a case by issuance of subpoenas for witnesses, then going to a grand jury and possibly a pre-trial. Witnesses must be interviewed to be certain what they are going to testify and to evaluate the impact that their testimony may have on the case. Witnesses cannot, however, be forced to testify against themselves. Legal issues must be examined regarding points of law that may be presented to argue admissibility of evidence. Search warrants can be used to seize evidence. In the case of the prosecutor, all of this must be done within time constraints that will permit the constitutionally guaranteed speedy trial. Defense attorneys will often press for a quick trial so as to give the prosecution inadequate time to prepare.

With a civil trial, the preparation consists of assembling every scrap of evidence that can be put together. The process is called discovery. The rules of discovery permit a broad inquiry that will allow attorneys for both sides to know everything about the case before the trial. Copies must be made available for all records requested by the opponents and the opponent must supply full records in return. Legal experts say that the use of discovery is one of the great abuses of the legal process.

Depositions, principally a process of civil law, are used to learn in advance what a person would testify at a trial. Depositions are used for criminal trials only when it is feared that a witness may not be available at the time of trial, either because of impending death or expected absence from the jurisdiction at the time of the trial. In a civil trial, a witness can be forced to testify against his or her own interest.

Subpoenas can be issued for a pretrial deposition. The subpoena requires the witness to appear at a designated place and time, with or without an attorney. The witness must provide the evidence that he will give at the trial. The deposition can be videotaped but a certified court reporter must take down every question, every answer, the exchanges between attorneys, every aside so that the person conducting the deposition can obtain a complete story of everything that the witness knows about the case.

A deposition serves several purposes. First, it puts the witness on record and if the witness testifies differently at the trial, than he has done at the deposition, then he is guilty of perjury. If the witness, is unable to attend trial then the record of the deposition will be used. If a witness gives false testimony at a trial, he can be impeached by producing evidence of what he said under oath. When a witness's testimony is attacked in this manner, a jury is not likely to believe the witness.

Commonly, if a trial involves serious financial issues, witnesses are inclined to either exaggerate or minimize the truth, however it may serve the purposes of that testimony. Yet, witnesses are not likely to expose themselves to charges of perjury.

Subpoenas may bring forth 50,000 pages of accounting records, videotapes, logs, correspondence, and the like. The attorneys pour through those documents for months with the use of specialists to find support for their case. Jurors would commonly be unable to understand the meaning of the majority of the documented records.

Then the attorneys search the law books for support for their case. Most beginning lawyers for firms spend their early years in the law libraries studying case after case. Every past case that bears a similarity to the current case must be studied and analyzed for principles that may be useful.

Then the briefs must be prepared. A brief is written study made about various points of law on anything that the attorneys believe may become an issue in the trial. A trial judge in a civil trial may have his desk covered with stacks of briefs that should be read.

If the case goes to trial, a unanimous verdict is not normally required. A consensus by a specified number of jurors, normally about nine, is considered sufficient.

In civil law, there is no such thing as something needing to be proven beyond a reasonable doubt. The juror need merely be convinced by the preponderance of evidence.

If the case is a litigious case, two types of monetary awards may be the decision of the jury and or judge. The damage award is intended to compensate the injured plaintiff to the extent of damages that he has suffered. Those damages may be physical, psychological, monetary or whatever the plaintiff's lawyer can add.

When a defendant is found to be guilty and, in theory, if the conduct was committed intentionally and with malice, an award can be made to the plaintiff for punitive damages. The idea is that this will punish the defendant and discourage others from committing the same offense or a similar one. In practice, this rule of law is the most abused of all rules because hundreds of huge damage awards are assessed when the circumstances that were involved in the guilty conduct were in no way intentional and were totally without malice.

The plaintiff must present proof that the defendant has the financial resources to be able to pay the amount of the judgment.

A civil trial is long, tedious, boring and generally uninteresting to the public. It certainly provides no incentive for coverage by the news media. Civil suits do not sell newspapers.

Are we to assume that in a civil case, the functioning of lawyers may be less subject to criticism than criminal law?

The following comes from a book of fiction but it was written by a lawyer who has become a famous author. The conditions which he described are confirmed by innumerable written articles that presume to offer factual information. So why not use the best available description?

The pattern commonly practiced by attorneys for large firms was described by John Grisham, author of "The Firm', "The Pelican Brief". "The Client" and many others.

"Most good lawyers can work eight or nine hours a day and bill twelve. It's called padding. It is not exactly fair to the client, but it's something everybody does. The great firms have been built by padding files. It's the nature of the game.

"Some of the most unethical people I know have been my own clients. It's easy to pad a file when your client is a multimillionaire, who wants to screw the government and who wants to do it legally. We all do it."

"You just sort of learn it. You'll start off working long crazy hours but you can't do it forever. So you start taking shortcuts. Believe me, after you've been with us a year, you'll know how to work ten hours and bill twice that much. It's a sixth sense that we all acquire."

"This business works on you. When you were in law school, you had some noble idea of what a lawyer should be. A champion of individual rights: a defender of the constitution, an advocate of your client's principles. Then after you practice for six months, you realize we are nothing but hired guns - mouthpieces available for sale to the highest bidder, available to anybody, any crook, any sleazebag with money enough to pay our outrageous fee. Nothing shocks you. It's supposed to be an honorable profession, but you'll meet so many crooked lawyers that you'll want to quit and find an honest job. Yeah, you'll get cynical. It's sad, really."

I am sure to be criticized for quoting from a book of fiction to confirm that it is as John Grisham has written but, although not stated in clear and precise forms by other writers, the accumulated descriptions are the same. Grisham practiced criminal law in Mississippi and served two terms in the Mississippi House of

Representatives. Then he became an author. He knows the profession of law.

As another exercise in padding, my daughter worked as a paralegal for a law firm that was working in support of another legal firm on one of the largest law suits to be litigated in the United States. She was frequently required to thermocopy documents to be presented to opposing law firms as part of the process of discovery. Oft times, the material to be copied was known to have no bearing on the case but by sending thousands of pages of extraneous documents, it became necessary for the opposing law firm to devote thousands of hours going through superfluous documents to be certain that no shred of useable material was hidden away in the inner pages. The opposing firm then returned the favor by transmitting untold pages of documents also having no bearing on the case. Thus, the billable hours built up on both sides as the clients paid for the superfluous hours. It was all done with intent and is a common practice within opposing law firms.

In another similar instance, after thousands of pages of thermocopied pages had been submitted to the opposing law firm, the message would come back that a large portion of the material was unreadable. This was done even though it was my daughter's judgment that there was not a single word that could be misread. Her own firm returned the favor by declaring great quantities of the opposition's material to be unreadable. The heavy volume of paper work was then recopied and charged to opposing firm at thirty dollars per hour while paying the paralegal little more than the minimum wage.

There was more. With the client paying the bills, if a simple eraser was purchased, ten copies of every invoice were made and transmitted to every member of the opposing law firm. With copy work being charged at one dollar per sheet, a simple 29 cent eraser could go into the billing system to the client at ten dollars for copying and 29 cents for the eraser, a total of at least $10.29.

To review Justice John Kane's expression of that same problem, he stated,

"In 1938 when the current code was written, when copies were made with carbon paper on manual operated typewriters, the inspection and copying of documents was a reasonable means of obtaining information. Today's practices, however, of sifting through warehouses filled with documents, copying hundreds of thousands of pages and offering into evidence as many as twenty or thirty thousand pages is nothing more than mindless ritualism...The average, personal injury case is over-discovered, over-briefed and over-tried as well."

Judge Kane failed to mention that the practice of filing tons of evidence makes impossible and meaningless the job of the jury. They do not have the capability to read and understand the endless documents that are dumped on them.

Abuse by lawyers is not limited to criminal cases.

Chapter 8

A Minor Case in Civil Law

Here, we have a case of litigation that is such a thorough miscarriage of procedure and results that the case must be camouflaged. Certain participants in the case stand to be penalized severely for speaking the truth since release of information violates the final settlement. Nevertheless, the actions are accurate.

We will suggest that this case is one in which a different brother-in-law, (let's call him Reggie) came into ownership of a large sum of money from a settlement with a trucking company when he couldn't get his vehicle out of the way fast enough. He accepted the proffered amount rather than filing a lawsuit under which he undoubtedly would have received much more. He admitted that he was rash about money decisions and, apparently he valued my judgment because he vowed that he would never invest a single dollar without asking my approval. He couldn't hold himself to that guideline as he frequently got into deep water and then asked for my help after the fact. The following case is one of those experiences.

Reggie agreed to a working relationship that had the potential to cost him dearly. Just for perspective, although I cannot guess at an actual amount, I would say that Reggie's financial resources may have been in the vicinity of two million dollars, but by the time I knew about the deal, there was a likelihood that essentially all of his assets might be seriously jeopardized This is legal process, maybe not at its very worst, but close enough to the worst to illustrate a great hazard.

In 1986, Reggie was introduced to trouble, one of three brothers that he met in a bar and later, through that brother, he not only met the other two brothers but also met Archie Marable, a promoter of business opportunities. Marable had already approached the three brothers with a proposal that they form a general partnership to make a very advantageous investment. Marable would be a fourth investor and he believed that it was advisable to add a fifth to bring financial backing to the needed level. The brothers recommended their new friend Reggie to round out the partnership and each of the five could be expected to net a sizeable profit without putting any cash into the venture. With the surname of the three brothers being Bethune, the partnership would operate as the Bethune Partnership.

A total of $750,000 was needed to finance the endeavor, not a large sum among investors, but enough to support installation of an automated storage and retrieval equipment system in a specialized warehouse in Fort Worth, Texas. The supplier of the system was known as Automated Systems, Inc. As explained by Marable and as confirmed by representatives of the warehouse company, the equipment had, in initial operations, functioned very effectively for more than a year. Cash flow documents had been presented for examination by the prospective partners.

Marable, the promoter, would sign a note with the bank for the required amount of financing and all of the five partners would co-sign the loan that would guarantee repayment. That, although no lawyer had explained the facts to them, pledged the entire assets of each of the five men. Archie Marable would act as general manager for the partners.

With everything apparently in order, the contracts were signed on July 1, 1987 and Automated Systems, Inc. completed the transaction by sale of the storage and retrieval system to the partnership. The partnership was now the owner of an automated storage system and it was leased to Modern Hygienic Storage, operator of the warehouse. In most respects, this was a typical method of financing high priced operating equipment.

The monthly lease payments began arriving and they were sufficiently large that they could be expected to amortize the loan, plus pay interest and yield an excellent profit for each of the investors. What a sweet investment!

When Archie Marable became a member of the Bethune Partnership, he was increasing his own beneficial rewards from the deal because he was also a principal share owner and member of the board of directors of Modern Hygienic Storage. Marable purported to be showing sufficient faith in his own enterprise to share the opportunity with the investors and that reinforced their comfort level.

Then, fifteen months after the partners had signed a contract, and regular dividends had been received, the partnership members were shocked when Modern Hygienic Storage suddenly disconnected the equipment and entered a demand that the equipment should be removed immediately. An investigation, more thorough than before, disclosed that the high-tech equipment had never performed satisfactorily, and indeed at the very time that the partnership had been persuaded to sign the contract for ownership, a rupture had been developing between Archie Marable and other members of management at Modern Hygienic Storage.

Fraud had apparently been committed by Marable and other executives of the operating company. Outsiders had been induced to provide financing at the very time that they, as owners and officers of the operating company, were representing to the partnership that everything was functioning properly.

This clearly called for an attorney to represent Reggie and the three brothers. Reggie proposed hiring a prominent law firm in Dallas but he was outvoted and, since they had, without telling him, already paid a retainer to an attorney named Kurt Sondreau, he accepted their decision. This was a member of a two-man law partnership who was willing to take the effort on a contingency basis.

In our subject case, a lawsuit was soon filed in January, 1989 in Texas state court charging Archie Marable and Modern Hygienic Storage with fraud. The suit demanded return of the unpaid balance of the bank loan, originally $750,000, plus interest and certain expenses.

Modern Hygienic Storage quickly filed a countersuit in federal court claiming that the equipment which had been installed by Automatic Systems, but which was now owned by the Bethune Partners, had done $60,000 worth of damage to ancillary equipment to which it was connected.

Within a few months, the bank also failed as one of the nationwide wave of bank closings. Now the liability was not to the bank but to the Federal Deposit Insurance Corporation, the branch of the federal government that oversees banking operations. The initial suit was transferred to federal court.

With suit and countersuit now in federal court, Archie Marable promptly declared himself bankrupt to place himself out of reach of either lawsuit. This also relieved him of having to make payments to the bank on any share of the $750,000 loan.

We Americans make certain assumptions about our court system. A judge would never punish a client for inappropriate actions by his attorney. Every person is entitled to a day in court. We all have a right to swift settlement of legal disputes. Right? Wrong on all counts.

After the suit and countersuit had been filed, nothing happened and the sheets steadily drifted off the calendar. Finally in March 1990, the court ordered that certain pre-trial papers were required to be filed no later than May, 1991, 14 months in the future. Then, on an intermediate date of March, 1991, attorneys for Modern Hygienic Storage filed a motion to throw Bethune's suit out of court.

When the date arrived, it was learned that Sondreau had still forgotten to file the required papers. A month later, the attorney for the warehouse company again filed a motion for the partnership's case to be thrown out of court. Finally, in April, Sondreau responded with a claim that they could not go to trial because with the bankruptcy of Archie Marable, his status blocked Sondreau from obtaining a necessary deposition from him. No effort had been made, however, to obtain permission from the bankruptcy judge to depose Marable.

In December 1991, the judge complied with the requests from the attorney for Modern Hygienic Storage and entered a judgment that threw the partnership's claim out of court. Provision was made, however, that the action could be appealed by February 28. Kurt Sondreau responded by forgetting to file notice of appeal by that new required date.

The judge's action of December eliminated the lawsuit that the partners had filed for $750,000 plus costs but left intact the countersuit for $60,000 against the partnership. It also established conditions that since the attorney had failed to file papers including the list of witnesses by the due date of March, 1991, no witnesses would be permitted to testify in behalf of Bethune.

During the period when so many required filings were being missed from the initial date of May, 1991 to the date of the final climactic crushing blow of November 20, 1992, the partnership received no word from it's attorney that anything was amiss except that he repeatedly told them that everything was proceeding satisfactorily and that they were just waiting for a date on the docket.

The judge's action of November set a pre-trial conference for December 19, 1992 and it was learned that Sondreau still had not filed the pre-trial papers that had been due almost a year and a half earlier. Further, he arrived late for the conference and the judge was visibly angry.

In trial before the judge, the Bethune Partnership was denied the opportunity to submit evidence. No witnesses for the defense were admitted to the stand. Surprise! In a trial before the judge without a jury and without witnesses for the defendants, the judge rendered a decision for the countersuit on the basis of incomplete evidence from Modern Hygienic.

To get a most accurate description of the impact of the Judge's decision, let's go to the subsequent summation by the Court of Appeals:

"As a penalty for counsel's failure to comply with the filing deadlines, the district court struck (Bethune's) pleadings in defense of (Modern Hygienic's) counterclaim, granted (Modern Hygienic's) default judgment on the issue of liability, and ordered a hearing three days later on the damages.

"At the damages hearing on September 1, 1993, despite the fact that (Modern Hygienic's) pleadings requested damages of not less than $60,000, the district court entered judgment in favor of (Modern

Hygienic) for $592,000 in actual damages, $328,000 in prejudgment interest, and $90,000 in attorney's fees."

It was stated very clearly that, "As a penalty for defendant's counsel's failure to comply,…" The client was being punished for the sins of the counsel, not the amount of $60,000 that plaintiff had requested but a judgment that immediately totaled $1,760,000 plus any interest that would accrue during any appeals process.

The next devastating occurrence was that two of the three brothers in the partnership took refuge in bankruptcy to protect themselves from the judgment. Although he had given no indication of doing so, the probability existed that the third brother would do the same.

For any reader who might be considering becoming a member of a general partnership, there should be a warning that there are three types of business organization. In a sole proprietorship, the single operator receives all of the benefits from the business and is responsible for every debt of the business. With a corporation, the benefits from the business belong to the stockholders who are the owners but those stockholders are normally protected from individual responsibility for debts of the corporation.

The potential investor must beware of the general partnership, the third of the forms of business. The benefits from the partnership are to be divided among the members according to the partnership agreement but if a judgment should be rendered against the partnership, each and every partner can be held individually and totally responsible for all liabilities of the partnership. Thus, in a partnership involving five people, all would share in the profits according to the agreement that formed the partnership, but if there are debts, each individual is totally responsible that all debts are paid in full. Thus if four of the five partners were to declare bankruptcy, the fifth and remaining partner may well find himself liable for 100% of the debts of the partnership even if it requires all of his owned assets to settle the indebtedness.

In the lawsuit of Modern Hygienic, Inc vs Bethune Partnership, the two remaining partners, my brother-in-law and one brother, severed ties with Sondreau and partner, and soon began to learn more about their former counsel. With new, competent counsel now representing them, an investigation was begun.

The first lawyer, Kurt Sondreau, claimed to have been ill during the period of the proceedings. He was subsequently diagnosed as having a form of diabetes that causes extensive loss of memory.

This diabetic lawyer, had in several proceedings, been represented by his partner but in many instances, there had been no communication between the two on occurrences that had transpired. Unknown to the men of the partnership, the second lawyer had never been admitted to the bar in the applicable District of Texas. Still later, it was learned that this second attorney had been on disciplinary probation by the Texas State Bar for cocaine dependency.

A new appeal was filed on the basis of inadequate legal representation by the newly hired prestigious law firm from Dallas. The district court (the same judge that had rendered the earlier judgment) heard the appeal and denied appeals in regard to both lawyers. In the case of Sondreau, the denial was on the basis that in spite of the claimed disease, he had still proceeded with other cases. The denial in regard to the second lawyer was without explanation.

Now the Bethune Partnership (of two remaining members) had a judgment against them of $1,010,000 plus a legal duty to repay the loan that had originated from the bank but was now property of FDIC and had been guaranteed for $750,000 plus interest. The governmental agency was steadily adding interest to the guaranteed loan. What had once been a loan guarantee amounting to $150.000 per investor in the partnership was now nearing $1,200,000 for each of two remaining investors and was still climbing with accruing interest.

My brother-in-law stood the possibility of holding sole responsibility for the entire huge debt. With the total of the judgment, bank loan, and interest now past $2,000,000, it exceeded his total assets. If one more brother availed himself of bankruptcy and if the judgment stood, Reggie would have had no option but to also take refuge in bankruptcy. His assets would not cover the juggernaut of exploded costs.

Finally, appeal was made to the U.S. Court of Appeals on the basis that all judgments should have been rendered on the merits of the case and not on failure of counsel to follow proper legal procedures.

In a case of January 12, 1995, a form of justice was finally decreed.

1. "The appeal to reinstate the original lawsuit against Modern Hygienic Storage was denied basically because of the expiration of too much time after the judgment before the next legal action. 'Excusable neglect' would have been a valid reason for reinstatement but the illnesses of the two attorneys did not constitute "excusable neglect."

2. The district court should have imposed a less severe sanction than granting a default judgment on the basis of liability for several reasons considered cumulatively. First, the sanction was too severe, given the lawyer's conduct...Second, there is no evidence that the district court considered imposing less severe sanctions than default. Third, an available lesser sanction would have been a sufficient and appropriate penalty in this case."

Finally, the court wrote, "While recognizing that a party is bound by the acts of his lawyer-agent, and may suffer dismissal with prejudice if his counsel is chargeable with clear delay or contumacy, the proper punishment for an inept lawyer is to assess fines, attorney's fees, or costs against the lawyer without harming the client. In summary, since no delay or prejudice resulting from the attorney's inaction and lesser sanctions would have been sufficient, the punishment did not fit the crime in this case."

As a final conclusion to this case, the decision by the Appeals Court laid the basis for a new trial on the $60,000 countersuit. Since witnesses would be allowed to testify and documentary evidence would be permitted to be entered into evidence, the partnership had little doubt that they would triumph in a new trial with competent legal representation.

Primarily, there was the matter for Reggie and his wife that the stresses of seven years of legal battle had exacted a heavy mental and physical toll. They had been threatened with loss of every thing that they owned except what they would be permitted to retain by the laws of bankruptcy. Severe problems had developed in the digestive tract for Reggie and his wife was also showing wear and tear from the drawn out process. Freedom from those stresses was something that must be considered.

Secondly, there was the matter of legal costs. The Dallas legal firm who would handle the new case would not come cheaply. A minimum fractional payment was offered for settlement by the partnership and accepted by Modern Hygienics Storage.

In total, it was a sorry experience with the legal profession. There was absolutely no penalty for Archie Marable, the original perpetrator of improper contract compliance and conflict of interest. Nor was the judge in any way reprimanded. Nor was there any real punishment for the lawyer who was incompetent, negligent and fraudulent.

Author of the book, *The Terrible Truth about Lawyers*, Mark H. McCormack described the nature of Reggie's experience:

> "Lawyers work inside a wall of molasses. Molasses is gummy, slow, and more or less opaque. Once you have made contact with the wall of molasses, you can't move up. You can't move down and you can't move from side to side. You usually can't even get back out again.
>
> "Anyone who has ever been involved in even the most routine legal procedure can testify how exhausting it is to make progress through that wall."

In Reggie's case, the "entrenched nobility" will proclaim that justice finally triumphed, that it shows the validity of the total judicial process. But when we consider the legal costs that were generated and the amount of emotional stress encountered by various members of the cast, the cost was heavy indeed. The case had not been without further impacts. Reggie and his wife suffered severe health deterioration under the stresses of the seven year ordeal.

But, the lawyers will say that this case was an aberration, a one time example of what can happen when there are bad apples in every barrel. In general practice, the legal process will work on a much higher level of competence.

This case has been presented to show the complexities that can develop with a minor case of civil law.

Chapter 9

Twin Fountains of Wealth - Sprinkler and Fire Hose

Two giants scams have been created by lawyers but, being lawyers, they have been created in an entirely lawful manner and indeed the scams are operated as part of the legal process. They provide two great pipelines from the consumer, particularly from the insurance buying public, to the lawyers. They are, first, the class action lawsuits and, secondly, the punitive damage awards against corporations, and such high priced practitioners as surgeons, medical doctors, and anesthesiologists. And, oh yes, even against lawyers. Often the class action lawsuits and the claims for punitive damages are combined in a single lawsuit with greatest effectiveness. They provide money in unbelievable quantities for the attorneys who practice in these fields.

A system of litigation to benefit the lawyers!

The class action half of the tandem is like a giant sprinkler with a rupture in the vertical stem. Money flows out through that opening in great volume to provide attorneys with massive funds.

In the other part of the pattern, the money flowing from the rotating sprinkler arm is scattered so widely that it makes no more contribution to the irrigation of the field than enough to settle the dust – er – of almost unnoticeable benefit to the financial well being of the unnumbered plaintiffs.

As this chapter is being written, I am waiting for the arrival of a check with my share of one class action lawsuit. The cause was truly just and is one where the defendants in the suit should have made proper payments.

I own certain oil royalty rights, not enough to represent wealth but large enough that the payments help. The oil and gas wells are past their prime in quantity of production. My total income from the royalty rights falls between $1000 and $1500 each year. My wife owns more royalty rights than me so her income adds to about four times as much. Still, that is not enough to place us among the wealthy.

Five oil companies were producing oil from wells on miscellaneous properties and they had committed a form of fraud that, for a long period, had gone undetected. Each month, we royalty owners had been sent a tabulated statement showing the amount of oil and gas that has been produced from the property whose rights we own, and a listing of the price for which the product has been sold. Then when the total income from each well was calculated, I personally have been entitled to about a quarter of one per cent (.0025) of the total value of all production from the wells in which I held an interest. Yes, that is the source of the thousand dollars per year.

The fraudulent action was that instead of selling the oil on the open market at the current market price as should lawfully have been done, these companies had formed subsidiary companies and had sold the oil to those subsidiaries for something less than the market price. Then the subsidiaries sold the oil and gas at the market price for a profit. It was a small bit below the market price and with the shortfall spread amongst thousands of royalty owners, it had gone unnoticed. Still, with all of the oil being produced by five companies from dozens of wells, the matter became a target for alert attorneys. The lawyers filed suit to make the oil companies pay for the shortfall in dollars, a total that would add to many millions.

The analysis of production from so many wells and so many property owners required hundreds of thousands of hours of labor by the attorneys, accountants and paralegals.

My brother, my cousin and I each have made guesses as to how large our checks would be. The guesses averaged about $12 each. Possibly there wont be any checks at all since we are well past the date on which the law firm said the checks would be issued. The payments to us, as members of a class of plaintiffs, has been delayed time after time and it is a certainty that the fees to the attorneys are growing with every passing day.

The attorneys are collecting four and a half million dollars in fees. Except for the fact that they undoubtedly performed and charged us hundreds of dollars per hour for much work that didn't actually need to be done, there is nothing immoral nor unethical about what they did, but there wasn't any real incentive for us to want the case to go to court. Yet, the attorneys added a great deal to their wealth.

The lawyers have used the law to correct an actual wrong but who knows how many hours will have been charged at $250 per hour or how many thousands of hours of paralegal time will have been charged to the case at $30 per hour while paying those workers the minimum wage. The legal costs will all have been charged to the case and that means that it will come out of the pool of money designated for us who are plaintiffs. The plaintiff money, however, is before expenses and when expenses have been paid, we find that the pool of money has evaporated down to a wetted bottom. (The reader should remember this case because the results will be described at the end of this chapter.)

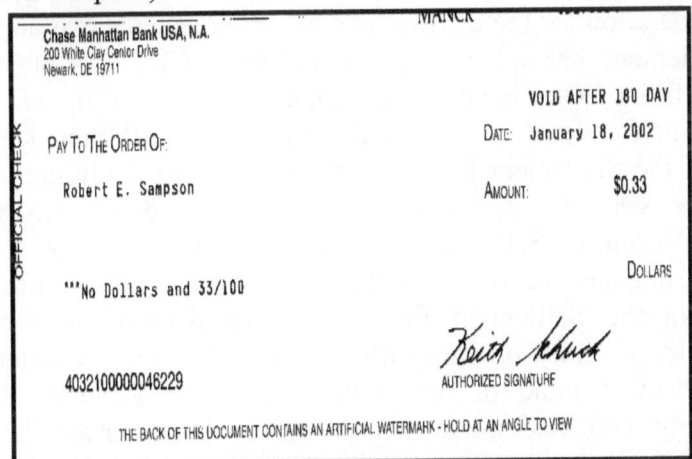

Figure 9-1 Check in full settlement of a class action lawsuit

When my brother received the pictured check in full payment for being one of a class of plaintiffs in one lawsuit for which the lawyers received millions, there was no concern about the bank being able to cash his check. He did, however, save the check as an exhibit.

When I started writing this book, I thought I knew how bad the situation was but as I read more and more books, I learned that it is several times worse than I understood. Instead, of five chapters on the subject, a total book on litigation would have been appropriate.

In fact, Walter K. Olson has published two of the most important books of the decade. The titles are: *The Litigation Explosion What Happened When They Unleashed the Lawsuit* and *The Rule of Lawyers – How the New Litigation Elite Threatens America's Rule of Law*. These books are available from Simon & Schuster and are supplemented by Olson's web site www.overlawyered.com.

Today, I received notification of settlement of a different lawsuit of which I had not previously been aware. The lawyers don't bother to obtain agreement from the group of persons whom they claim to have been injured as a cause for their lawsuit.

The following statement will help the reader understand how the settlement statements are written so as to minimize the amount received by the plaintiff member and how that money is instead channeled to the lawyers.

"(Blank Company), in settlement of the claims of this action, and in consideration for the releases and other agreements that are part of this settlement, has agreed to pay the Plaintiff Class the total sum of Three Million, One Hundred thousand dollars ($3,100,000.00) (the Settlement Fund)…Class Counsel will seek an attorney fee of *33 1/3%* of the Settlement Fund and reimbursement for litigation costs and expenses. If approved by the court, these amounts will be deducted from the Settlement Fund prior to distribution to the class. (Blank Company) in addition will bear the cost of notice to the Class and from the Settlement Fund and administration of the Class settlement. (Blank Company) will be entitled to reimbursement from the Settlement Fund of up to *$250,000.00 in expenses* that are reasonably and necessarily incurred in administering the Class Settlement. If the Settlement is finally approved by the court at the scheduled Fairness Hearing, each member of the Settlement Class will be paid according to a plan of allocation approved by the court. The plan of allocation will be designed to distribute to Settlement Class Members their respective proportionate share of the Settlement Fund based generally on the size of the royalty owner's interest and the volume of (Blank Company) gas sold during the pertinent time frame. The portion of the Settlement Fund <u>to be paid to each Settlement Class Member will be reduced by that Settlement Class Member's allocation of Class Counsel fees, and any litigation expenses, class representatives fee and all expenses incurred in the administration and distribution of the Settlement Fund.</u>

Three legal firms will receive $1,033,333.33 plus expenses and costs. Figure the hourly rate at $250 or more per hour and reproduction costs at a dollar a page and then would anyone care to wager that I will get even ten cents from the Settlement Fund? Who did this law suit benefit?

I own only a moderate number of stocks and also have royalty rights from three wells. From those, I have been notified by a legal firm about half dozen times that I am a member of a class in whose behalf a class action lawsuit has been filed. I normally am required to sign a form and return it if I wish to be exempted from the class. Often I am called on to provide other detailed information, much of which I don't have in my files. In one case that I remember, I was required to return receipts for any purchases, receipts of a nature that no homeowner retains, if I wanted to be recompensed at a few cents on the dollar.

As a first problem, the documents are all written in complex legal terms which would make it necessary for me to hire a lawyer to analyze the claims. Most of the paragraphs are boiler plate with which the attorneys are familiar and through which I have no desire to take hours to examine. If you put in a call to the legal firm, it invariably takes weeks to receive a response with the information that the answers are not yet available.

The class action may be of healthy benefit to the owner of millions of shares of stock but for those with limited investments, the benefit will not justify the expenditure of time required to establish one's position. But while I simply avoid putting forth the effort because of inadequate time, the lawyers rake in the millions of dollars. The class action suit sounds heroic and makes a great favorable segment on the evening news but the benefits fall among the ashes.

In recent litigation, Jim Branson sued several of the automobile manufacturing companies claiming infringement on his patent for intermittent windshield wipers. Branson finally won his suit against Chrysler and received a compensatory award of eleven million dollars for violating his patent. Attorney fees were approximately 8 ½ million dollars. Other costs consumed most of the remaining 2 ½ million dollars which had been intended to go to the individual whose rights had been violated.

When the class action suit involves punitive damages the results will continually build up the wealth of the legal firms. Consider the Exxon Valdez case where the captain of an oil tanker was drunk and caused the ship to run onto a reef with great damage to the bay. A generous jury provided a verdict of $287 million dollars in compensation for losses and a punitive verdict of 5 billion dollars. Although the legal fees haven't been announced, the first estimate was that they would be about 400 million dollars. Exxon took the case to the Court of Appeals and that court ruled that the punitive damages were unreasonably high. So guess what! The case is still continuing 12 years after the spill and two things are happening. The fisherman who were affected by the spill and in whose name the suit was filed are dying off and will never receive any of the benefits from the lawsuit and, secondly, the coffers of the lawyers are filling higher and higher with each day of accumulated hours in the lawyers' office.

Inventors and engineers have always fantasized that they would invent a machine that achieves perpetual motion. This would be a machine of 100 per cent efficiency. The energy that comes out of the machine as work would be precisely equal to the energy that drives the machine so that, once started not one extra erg of work would be required to operate the machine. No additional energy would have to be fed into the machine to keep it operating. They know that this cant happen because it defies the logic of energy usage.

My friend, Richard Gauthier, now deceased, jokingly contended that he would design a machine that would be the opposite of perpetual motion. Every B.T.U. of energy would be consumed as friction with the end result being that not one unit of useful work would come out of the machine. Dick's reference to a zero efficiency machine was intended as a satirical comparison to many governmental operations.

The lawyers have, however, achieved zero efficiency in an enormous class action lawsuit filed against General Motors. The lawyers nominally represented 5.7 million pickup truck owners in 49 states. The truck owners were overwhelmingly pleased with their trucks and found no fault with them. But when the pot started boiling under a Georgia lawsuit that resulted in a $105 million jury award, General Motors offered a settlement that pleased both the lawyers and General Motors. GM would achieve a marketing triumph and the lawyers would receive 21 million dollars in fees for representing the owners who had no desire to be represented. GM agreed to send a $1000 coupon to each truck owner as liability compensation with the coupon to apply to the purchase of a next pickup truck.

We are familiar with coupons as one of the most ubiquitous marketing tools in existence and that was how GM saw the coupons that were sent to truck owners. For GM, the coupons could help serve the first big need of automobile marketing and that was to get the potential buyer into the show room.

Normally, General Motors would spend many dollars for each truck that they hope to sell on such diverse advertising venues as television, radio, magazines, and billboards. For a time, all of those expenditures could be cut back because the customers would be brought into the show rooms by the $1000 coupons.

On a typical coupon intended for use in a grocery store, a 75 cent coupon will usually carry a notice that the cash value of the coupon is worth one twentieth of a cent. On the same ratio, the $1000 coupon for a truck would be worth 67 cents. Haven't you, the reader, received $1000 simulated checks to be valid only when applied on the purchase of a vehicle from a certain automobile dealer? Those are $1000 coupons worth about 67 cents in cash.

In addition, automobile dealerships always quote a price that is several thousand dollars higher than the price for which they are willing to sell the vehicle. Those thousands of dollars provide room for negotiation and it is the astute buyer who can trim that margin to the minimum. So the 67 cent coupon will have cost General Motors nothing except the normal costs of doing business.

General Motors would achieve a great marketing success. The lawyers gained $21 million in fees. In this case, the class-action plaintiffs gained nothing except an invitation to visit the showroom and a coupon that was worth about as much as most coupons, about 1/20 cents on the dollar. Dick Gauthier's zero efficiency system had been achieved with a $21 million dollar side benefit to the lawyers.

A different class action law suit was filed against General Motors brought on behalf of "all persons everywhere now alive and all future unborn generations" This surely was the highest amount ever demanded in a law suit as it sought six trillion dollars in damages from pollution. It has never been resolved.

Now we come to the most appalling activity in all of the legal repertoire, the punitive damages against the corporation. This is so bad because it is all built on a fiction. And the money comes gushing forth to the attorneys like water from an open six inch fire hose.

One of the strong passions of my life is a desire to have the corporations accepted with fairness by the world of public opinion but it isn't going to happen as long as we have the news media, the educational institutions and the labor unions all breaking the bonds of logic to spread a gospel that the corporations should be hated. My stand is not because I own a large quantity of corporate stock nor because any relative of mine has such a source of wealth, but rather because of an overriding sense of fairness.

The industrial corporations are largely responsible for giving Americans the highest standard of living in the world and they provide millions of jobs that drive our economy the world over. Further, the corporations provide a method by which every American who can save a few dollars from that weekly or monthly pay check can invest it to build a better economic future for the family. That was once the American dream.

I have heard all of the complaints about corporate greed and corrupt officers but I also know that most of the trash talk is hate propaganda. Certainly, there are pockets of unsatisfactory conduct in every corporation just as there are in every aspect of American life but a knowledgeable balance comes out far on the favorable side.

On the realistic side, the corporations have a far more difficult struggle making the profits that it needs to stay in business than the sources would have us believe. In 2002, for example, out of the 990 largest industrial corporations in the United States, over 25 per cent lost money instead of making a profit. With the steady stream of invective about the United States going to war in Iraq so that Halliburton Corporation could make big profits, the truth is that the company lost 984 million dollars in 2002. Almost a billion dollar loss!

Why my concern about the false propaganda about the corporations? The fiction that the corporations have such enormous wealth is a driving force behind the incredibly high punitive damage awards that are crippling the American economy. As long as the plaintiff's attorney can seat a jury who believes that the corporation being sued has deep pockets of incredible wealth, they can expect punitive damage awards of hundreds of millions of dollars with probably half of it going into the pockets of the extremely wealthy legal firm.

The assessments of punitive damages should be classified as hate-crimes. Attorneys for the plaintiff have done everything possible to select a jury that is inclined toward the hate-the-corporation mentality. Then, throughout the trial, they have been emphasizing the corruption that is represented by the situation that is at the center of the lawsuit. Finally there is the ever present message that the corporation must be punished for it's transgression. $100 million? $500 million? Could they make it a trillion? The omnipresent plea is that the jury must send a message to the corporation. The greater amount that the jury can be persuaded to assess as an appropriate penalty, the better job the jury has done in the eyes of the plaintiff. It is a matter of capitalizing on hatred. The lawyers are the ones that gain the most.

So the jury wants to send a message! Let's consider the Ford Pinto case where the jury was convinced that a single weld ruptured to cause the fire that in turn resulted in severe injuries for a young driver. It resulted in an award of $128,000,000. Who is going to receive the message and who will act on it? With 350,000 employees and thousands of machines, the message is spread so evenly that the automatic welder that made that particular weld has no doubt already been repaired or junked. Obviously, there has not been a pattern of consistent failures. The message is lost in the numbers.

The message is sent to the officers and directors of the company. The most they can do is to issue a directive to their insurance department that it must be certain that the company carries sufficient liability insurance. A higher level of liability insurance is then purchased. And guess what! The price of the liability insurance is added on to the price of future automobiles. Calculations were once made that liability insurance was adding $500 to the cost of every automobile. Today it is probably up to $1000. Now the cost of the penalty is being paid by the car-buying public. What happened to the concept that this was supposed to be punitive?

A second impact is that because of liability suits, many products have indeed been improved. Take the child's safety seats. For so many years, no matter what car seats were designed, they were soon "proven" to be unsafe with a potential for lawsuits that would result in giant punitive awards. Every parent wanted the child to be totally safe so no price for a car seat was too expensive to keep little Johnny protected. The cost of living becomes higher and higher. By the time that trend of responding to the punitive law suits is built in down through all the products of American manufacturing system, the cost of living has gone skyward.

Maybe the stockholders of the corporation will feel the brunt of the heavy punitive awards. In the case of the Exxon Valdez incident, when the verdict was announced, the price of a share of stock dropped $2.63 per share. Not a heavy message there.

Another impact of the punitive awards is the fact that numerous products have been taken off the market. A plastic had been developed which had great potential for use in hip replacement, and in tests, it seemed to have worked exceptionally well. But the manufacturer recognized the potential for liability suits, particularly their punitive awards, and took the plastic off the market. Those persons who needed hip replacements were deprived of what may have been their best option.

Vaccine makers have been sued so often with the concomitant punitive awards that most of them have gone out of business. The companies decide they are not going to innovate. Are a half dozen vaccine developers going to provide as many good vaccines as would have been provided if there were forty companies doing research on immunization?

Pacemakers cost $3000 more because of liability insurance. Football helmets cost $100 more. Even bread costs more. Every item of food costs more because of liability insurance.

Obviously, the cost of liability insurance strikes most heavily on those members of the buying public who are responsible enough and financially able to buy insurance. It also strikes, however, at those in the worst of poverty because it adds to the cost of a loaf of bread and to every item of food on all the tables of America, all of the medical bills, the cost of gasoline, the cost of clothing, the cost of education, and everything consumed by every resident of the country.

Surely, someplace there is a beneficial impact from the huge punitive awards. Yes, that goes to the attorneys.

Isn't there a plaintiff who was represented by the attorneys who is going to benefit by that large sum of money? Yes, although those persons have already received a large sum in compensatory damages and we need to ask how wealthy we need to make one of the victims. In the case of the Pinto automobile, the victims were given $3.5 million in compensatory damages for the death of one person and the very extensive injuries to another and then the jury added $125 million in punitive damages.

Again going to the Exxon Valdez case, Exxon commissioned a study that placed the cost of cleanup at $113 million but the defense attorneys convinced the jury that the amount should be $287 million. We aren't really concerned with that differences but we have to suspect that the hate-crime factor was at play in that latter calculation. $174 million here and $174 million there but that is insignificant compared to the $5 billion in damages defined as punitive damages.

From Grand Rapids, Michigan has come the announcement of what may be the most ridiculous judicial decision in the history of lawsuits We all recollect the talking Chihuahua dog who has appeared in commercials for Taco Bell. Two men, Thomas Rinks and Joseph

Shields, filed suit claiming that it had been their idea to use the Chihuahuas and maintained that they had reached a verbal agreement They claimed that, in that contract, Taco Bell stole the idea for an advertising campaign without paying the two men. There were no injuries and no intrusion on civil rights, - and it has often been said that verbal contracts are virtually worthless.

A friendly jury, no doubt one filled with corporation haters, awarded the two men $30.1 million dollars for that dog's appearance in the commercials. Now, the judge, apparently an even more avid corporation hater, says that was not enough. He added $11.8 million dollars in interest to post a total award of $41.9 million dollars.

Let's list the impact of a huge punitive damages awards:

- Hate crime offense, hatred, that is, against the corporation.
- Elimination of many beneficial products
- Redesign of products to make them more expensive and possibly of a better quality than we actually need.
- An increase in the cost of living for every resident of the nation
- A minimal impact on operations of the corporation that was the planned target of the lawsuit.
- **A giant sum of money for the lawyers.**

It is my personal opinion that the great punitive awards are the greatest evil in American society today, greater even in terms of money collected than the take of all of the criminal mobs and all of the drug rings in America.

Fortunately, some courts of appeal are repeatedly reducing the amounts of the punitive awards or sending them back to be recalculated at a more reasonable level.

In fact, it is not the individual punitive awards that hurt so much but it is the cumulative effect of the thousands of liability suits all of which include attempts to establish serious liability awards. The best estimate of total jury awards to date has been 200 billion dollars. Could that have an effect on our economy?

There is a simple and effective method by which the problems of the inappropriate punitive awards could be corrected. Let's pass a law that no part of punitive awards, when the jury elects to make such an award, shall go to either the plaintiffs or the attorneys. All monies from punitive awards should go into some project that would benefit the public. Possibly, a wise choice of projects for those funds would be one to improve the physical condition of all schools in the United States. Or to upgrade the physical facilities of the criminal justice system.

— ∎ — ∎ — ∎ — ∎ — ∎ — ∎ — ∎ — ∎ — ∎ — ∎ — ∎ —

Brookings Institute conducted a study to learn what potential products were being withheld from the marketplace because of anticipation of law suits which were almost certain to come if the product were launched. Typical of the products which could be launched except for the certainty of oncoming lawsuits with their punitive damages:

- Portable machine for kidney dialysis
- Newly designed flight training aircraft
- A safe substitute for asbestos
- Better child safety seats for the automobile
- Pesticide that does not damage food crops
- Chemical processes that speed decay of chemical wastes
- Device to allow handicapped people to drive
- In medical fields add the following:
- Vaccines for measles
- Vaccines for diphtheria, whooping cough and tetanus
- Safer, more effective birth control devices
- Cure for neurological conditions that cause blindness.

That list represents major improvements that could be made in our standard of living except that they are denied to the American people because of the threats of lawsuits.

— ∎ — ∎ — ∎ — ∎ — ∎ — ∎ — ∎ — ∎ — ∎ — ∎ — ∎ —

The author has just been notified that he is a member of a class of plaintiffs against Acceler8 Corporation for which the settlement allows that I will receive $8.50 per share of stock purchased between 6/1/1995 and 5/31/1999. With 150 shares, that would be $1275. But wait! There is that eternal clause that says "less legal expenses." (I received no money but $65 worth of stock.)

I would remind readers of the lawsuit described earlier in the chapter where my brother, cousin, and I estimated that we would receive awards on the order of $12 each from the oil companies for arranging sales of oil at too low a price. Now, writing six months later after awards from that law suit have been distributed, my wife just received her check for one dollar from the class action lawsuit. My check is never going to arrive because the lawyers informed me that no check would be written when the cost of writing it would be larger than the amount of the check.

Millions of dollars for the attorneys and not one penny for this injured plaintiff!

Chapter 10

The Ultimate Attack on Product Liability

In no other industry have lawyers attacked a prey with such clearly defined results as the assault on the small aircraft manufacturing industry. Records have been maintained on every individual unit of production and liability suits have been so numerous that they almost completely shut down he industry.

In 1978, the high point before the onslaught, the industry produced 17,032 small aircraft, a small airplane being defined as any plane that carried no more than 19 passengers. From 1979 to 1993, the number produced was less than a thousand per year reaching a minimum of 555 in the final year. With that drop in plane production, over 100,000 employees lost their jobs.

The industry was vulnerable because of several factors. With aircraft lasting longer than most other products, the laws were so written that the builder bore responsibility for design details of the aircraft even though maintenance and care may have been out of its hands for several decades. Some units had even crashed and been rebuilt, and yet the manufacturer was being held responsible. That meant that under laws then in existence, the manufacturer could be held liable for a component in the original design which was claimed to be responsible for the crash.

Secondly, from the beginning of English Common Law, a principle had ruled that for one party, in order to be liable to another, must be at fault. In recent decades, however, the rules began to change. Instead of identifying the party that was at fault, the new liability looked to the party with the deepest pockets. Most of the small aircraft were built by sizeable corporations and to persons of a type normally admitted to juries, the word corporation meant "deep pockets" and to the lawyers, deep pockets meant sue. And sue they did, sometimes suing manufacturers of lesser components that had been included on the aircraft. One manufacturer was forced to spend $10,000 in legal fees to prove that its product had not even been included on the aircraft that was the subject of the lawsuit.

Like many other manufactured products, designs of equipment used on airplanes evolve with each change being made to new models to incorporate the new designs. Lawyers were able to successfully claim that new designs of a component meant that the original design had been faulty and thus serve as a basis for another successful suit.

Finally, in all too many cases, an airplane crash meant the trauma of serious injury which gave attorneys a basis on which to build sympathy for a plaintiff. The size of the awards increased steadily, eventually going over one hundred million dollars per award.

The history of Beech Aircraft over a four year period is a clear example of what lawyers have done to the small aircraft industry. During that period, the National Transportation Safety Board investigated 203 crashes of aircraft which had been manufactured by Beech Aircraft and in each and every crash, they concluded without exception that every accident was attributable to normal causes – weather, faulty maintenance, pilot error or mistakes by air controllers. This safety board had assigned men and women who knew airplanes and flying.

That had not stopped the lawyers. They were quick to bring lawsuits in every one of those 203 crashes always claiming that the crash had been caused by faulty design or faulty construction by Beech. Beech was forced to defend against the suits with expensive legal talent and untold hours. The struggle of defending against these suits resulted in costs of an average of $530,000 for each crash. For 203 crashes, that was a total cost of $107 million dollars to battle dreamed up flaws when the true experts had judged Beech to be without blame in every crash.

In the courtroom, the testimony of experts from the National Transportation Safety Board created a logical defense that would have convinced any reasonable fair minded jury. In a trial, the matter of proving something as you would to a group of fair minded, well educated, unbiased jurors is one thing but the defenders were not playing to a jury best assembled to search for the truth. They were arguing before juries from which reason had been weeded out and on which emotion could make more impact than common sense.

A company cannot sell many airplanes if it has to add $530,000 to the price of every airplane to cover the cost of litigation that must be anticipated. The sale of aircraft manufactured in the United States dropped precipitously.

In one case, at an airfield about 20 miles from Albuquerque, Edward Cleveland crashed a 13 year old Piper Super Cub into a van parked in the middle of the runway. The van had been placed in that location by the owner of the airfield specifically to prevent Cleveland from taking off.

Cleveland and the company he worked for had a history of unsafe flying practices and the owner was denying permission to use the airport. A local savings and loan company had, however, hired Cleveland's company to produce a commercial advertisement showing a sailplane gliding gracefully in front of the nearby Sandia Mountains.

Instead of renting two aircraft, one to tow the glider and one to hold the camera equipment, Cleveland had decided to make do with one plane. He pulled the pilot's seat out of the two seater plane and instructed his crew to mount the camera in that space. The cameraman would shoot the footage while sitting with his back squeezed against the instrument panel. Cleveland would pilot the plan from the rear seat.

The airfield owner denied permission for Cleveland's group to use the airport and parked his van midway down the runway to prevent takeoff. Dawn was breaking and the lights of the van were on when Cleveland released the plane's brakes and started down the runway. He didn't make it and smashed his face into the steel camera mounted in front of him. Severe brain damage was the result.

His family first sued the airfield owner for parking the van on the runway and collected $300,000. But those pockets hadn't been deep enough. The lawyer contended that the aircraft design was defective because a person in the rear seat could not see out the front window (to see the van). Never mind that the cameraman sat in a position that blocked any view that the pilot might otherwise have had. The entire design of the Piper Super Cub had been approved by the Federal Aviation Authority, but the jury was convinced and awarded the family over a million dollars in damages.

That case gave impetus to the lawsuit parade as liability awards industry wide multiplied nine times in the next ten years. Piper had carried insurance on aircraft that it manufactured until 1987. Then it dropped all insurance because they could only buy $10 million dollar deductible. Two years later Piper went into Chapter 11 bankruptcy.

Possibly a record in lack of logic was achieved when a pilot flew into a tree in 1989 and Beech Aircraft, manufacturer of the plane was sued. The pilot was arriving at dusk and decided to fly beneath the clouds to get a look at the field. He was warned by the control tower against such an action but went down to tree level anyway. It cost Beech more than $100,000 in legal fees before the suit was dismissed.

A study showed that injured plaintiffs, that is, the persons in whose name the injuries were claimed, received only 17% of all money awarded by the court. While the number of aircraft manufactured dropped from 17,033 in 1977 to 999 in 1994, the number of lawsuits climbed from 25 to 214 in the same period. The average price of planes went from $100,000 to over $300,000.

With an important industry dying in the wake of a tidal wave of lawsuits, a consensus began to develop in Congress that something must be done to allow that industry to rebuild. In August 1994, the General Aircraft Vitalization Act was signed into law and that act changed the rules. After the law was enacted, no suit for death or injury could be filed more than 18 years after the plane or parts had been manufactured. Thirteen states have passed state laws which set that limit at a shorter period, in some cases as low as six years.

Those acts have in fact revitalized an entire Industry. With that law signed by President Clinton, small aircraft production immediately underwent a 20% increase in output in 1995 with a new plant being constructed in Independence, Kansas which alone has an output of 2000 planes per year. That one expansion more than doubled the total U.S. production in 1994. Since then the industry has flourished.

Chapter 11

All Out Assault on the Medical Profession

How bad is it? Dr. Irl Sell, an anesthesiologist who practiced in Phoenix, Arizona for a lengthy career, had totally enjoyed his many years in his highly respected field. During the 1980's, however, the cost of malpractice insurance was soaring. By 1990, that cost alone had reached more than $1000 per week. And when Dr. Sell took a month of vacation, he was required to continue making the payments on that insurance, even when he was fishing or hiking. But that wasn't the worst of it. For neurosurgeons, obstetricians and orthopedics, it was more than $2000 per week. But even that wasn't the worst of it.

Some insurance companies were so overwhelmed with lawsuits that in many instances, they never bothered to defend against the charges. It wasn't feasible for them to pay the costs of defending against the lawsuit. It was less expensive to simply settle with the plaintiffs even if it was an illogical claim, and increase the insurance rates for the doctor. The insurance companies have not been concerned with the fact that the settled suit is falsely damaging the reputation of the doctor, the target of the suit.

Those attorneys who choose to file lawsuits, sometimes simply play spin the bottle, pick out some target and file a flock of charges even without having any basis for the suit. After all, lawsuit specialists have developed lists of complaints being filed against various occupations or specialties. Then, in discovery, they can pour through every available record to build a case when they find some act that they can declare to be the basis for a lawsuit.

Surely, that is the worst of it...but it isn't. When lawyers sue, other lawyers stand ready to sue the lawyer who sued if he fails to claim every potential charge on the published list of possible complaints against that particular category of defendant. No matter that they have no evidence against the defendant for that particular act of malfeasance. They must sue on every listed charge or they may be charged with gross negligence. The reference for this particular practice comes from a description of the Product Liability Lawyer's Manual in David K. Olson's The Litigation Explosion.

For every action that a doctor performs, there is a lawyer waiting to file suit and claim malfeasance. When a woman fell off of a horse soon after her husband's death, and suffered pain in her chest, she was referred to Dr. Sell. Well aware of the propensity of lawsuits to follow every type of surgery, he was, as always, determined to do every procedure to the highest level of perfection.

He planned a nerve blockage on the side of the worst pain and explained to the woman that there is sometimes some discomfort after such a procedure. She agreed that he should proceed and all went well.

Later, similar severe pain developed on her other side and he repeated the explanation about the possibility of discomfort as an after effect. Again the woman requested that he proceed. This time, she was soon complaining of pain in an upper right rib cage area. An x-ray revealed a small quantity of air in the lung cavity, a common after effect of such nerve blockages.

She was admitted to the hospital for an overnight stay and Dr. Sell requested that she be examined by a thoracic surgeon. The small pneumothorax resolved spontaneously and the patient was sent home with instructions to return for a precautionary follow-up visit. She did not return and never suffered any future problems.

On the very day that the statute of limitations (three years) would expire, Dr Sell was notified that a lawsuit was being filed against him. The lawyer had completed all necessary court documents for the suit and by that action, the lawyer was giving himself 12 months to go through the records on Dr. Sell's work to find reasons for which he could be sued.

The lawyer had learned about the woman's discomfort after the blockage when he overheard a conversation at a party and he had not bothered to get her permission for the law suit. In fact, he would never get the woman's permission. He was very persistent in pursuing her signature, something which she had no wish to give because she had gotten from the nerve blockage precisely what she had sought, i.e., relief from her pain. Relentlessly, he sought her approval for the lawsuit to the extent of repeat visits to her home. Dr Sell later learned that the attorney had been so persistent in trying to persuade the patient to sue him, that she finally sold her home and moved her place of residence to an undisclosed location to get away from the lawyer.

Twelve months after the first notice of law suit, Dr. Sell received notice from the court that the discovery period for follow up action by the attorney had expired and the doctor was home free. That woman's consent to a lawsuit had not come easily.

The constant threat of lawsuits from any problem that might be encountered in taking care of a patient, the relentless rise in the cost of malpractice insurance and the ever increasing interference from the government and the medical insurance company in the overall practice of medicine caused Dr. Sell to retire from his much loved profession in 1990, sooner than he would have liked.

As I sought accounts of episodes where doctors had been attacked by lawsuits, I learned that many were quite anxious to tell me their story but they are living in fear. They were quick to ask that I not use their name because of the possibility that some lawyer would retaliate by filing a lawsuit even if they had been long retired. One doctor in Oklahoma said that when he goes on vacation or a conference, the first thing he always does on his return to his office is to go through his mail to see if there is any notice of a lawsuit having been filed.

That same doctor related his experience in the case of an 18 year old woman who came to the clinic reporting that she was suffering from a severe headache. The headache lasted for three days as the doctors directed that a cat scan, spinal tap, and other tests be performed to determine the cause. A ruptured aneurysm was discovered and the woman was kept in the hospital for four days before she died.

Soon a lawsuit had been filed in federal court to get the case out of state where they would be certain of no jurors friendly to the doctor. When the case came to trial, the plaintiffs were relying on the testimony of an "expert witness". Questioning developed the fact that the expert had performed his autopsy in a tool shed at the cemetery. Further along in the case, it was discovered that in the expert's diagnosis of the case, he had the direction of flow of blood reversed. The judge became so angry at the plaintiff's attorney that the attorney took the fifth amendment to avoid having to answer questions.

Lawyers aren't even required to have an act of malpractice for which they are suing. They can simply file suit against a doctor and then they have two years to go through the doctors records until they find a history of some procedure where they can claim the doctor did something wrong.

Nothing so totally demonstrates the damage to the practice of medicine than the matter that research has been so completely shut down. The essence of research that has built up the great techniques and practices that can save lives is that ideas must be tested. In the matter of a mitral valve transplant which would later extend the life of my first wife, for example, the procedures first had to be performed one patient at time with a calm expectation that not every transplant would be successful. One transplant at a time, the doctors had to learn what would work and what would not. Deaths were going to happen until the surgeons had perfected a safe procedure. Now, however, in the climate of a lawsuit for every failure, no surgeon in his right mind will perform the necessary repetitions until they have validated a set of procedures. Consequently, the research necessary to develop life saving procedures has to a great extent been terminated.

One internist in Oklahoma had a male patient with a severe aneurysm in the abdominal aorta. The prognosis was grim. Yet, there was a procedure of catheterization which had been originated in concept but on which research had only been done to develop a safe procedure in one east coast hospital. Lawsuits were a clear threat for any surgeon who tried to proceed with what amounted to trial and error. Would any surgeon make the attempt without a proven procedure?

Fortunately, that particular case had a successful ending when the Oklahoma doctor learned of a single surgeon who had spent time at the east coast hospital. That procedure has now become a proven procedure and has been performed repeatedly.

How many lives are going to be lost because the lawyers have put an end to needed research?

Wards of hospitals are being shut down almost weekly under the onslaught of the law suits. Last week the Maternity Ward of Mercy Hospital in West Philadelphia was closed. The prior week it was the trauma center for Las Vegas. Soon to come will be closure of the maternity ward at the Largo Medical Center near Tampa, Florida. In June, 2002, a survey released by the American Hospital Association disclosed that approximately 300 hospitals had cut down on various departments, most of them being obstetrics wards.

The states with the most critical situations are Nevada, Mississippi and Pennsylvania. A study by the University of Nevada disclosed that 40% of obstetricians in the Las Vegas area are planning to move their practice out of state. The same study showed that 76% of the city's obstetricians have been sued, and 40% have been sued three or more times. Anesthesiologists in Nevada are currently experiencing an increase in liability premiums of 40 to 75 per cent.

Dr. Donald J. Parmisano, secretary-treasurer of the American Medical Association has emphasized, "We need a system that insures fair compensation and puts an end to the liability lottery."

Twenty two counties and 600,000 residents in northern Mississippi have relied on the North Mississippi Medical Center but that hospital has been unable to find new doctors with the result that it may soon cut back on emergency services. Neurosurgeons are available only part time. If you sustain a head injury while in that region, you will have to sustain a one hour transport to either Memphis, Tennessee or Jackson, Mississippi. If you fail to survive that journey, you will have become one of the victims of the tidal wave of law suits.

To document the seriousness of the problem in finite numbers, the Concerned Citizens for Care based in Doylestown, Pa. conducted a study to determine the names of physicians in Pennsylvania who are taking action to discontinue high risk procedures, leaving their practices to move elsewhere for lower liability insurance rates or taking early retirement.

Pennsylvania's world class hospitals have been adversely affected by sharp increases in malpractice premiums as well. Units and clinics have closed. Residency programs have been lost.

Philadelphia and the four surrounding Pennsylvania counties, - Bucks, Montgomery, Delaware and Chester - may possibly be the most serious crisis area in the nation, but the area is selected to be presented here not for that reason, but because the most complete information is available. In every instance, the high cost of liability insurance was a principal factor. In those five counties, the following physicians have retired, moved out of state, or, sometimes in the case of obstetricians, simply eliminated their practice:

- 54 Obstetricians/Gynecologists
- 17 Orthopedic Surgeons. (One had practiced his specialty in the area for 22 years.)
- 5 General Surgeons have left the state or retired
- 1 Gynecological Surgeon resigned two weeks
  after being given resident's top award for being
  the best teacher in the Operating Room.
- 8 Neurosurgeons
- 7 Ear, Nose and Throat specialists
- 2 Oncologist/Hematologists
- 2 Urologists
- 4 Cardiovascular surgeons
- 7 Internists
- 3 Rheumatologists
- 2 Neurologists
- 8 Family Practice Physicians
- 4 Cardiologists
- 4 Gastroenterologists
- 2 Dermatologists

- 1 Pulmonologist
- 1 Emergency Department Director

For the total state of Pennsylvania, 244 medical personnel – surgeons, specialists, and technical people – announced that they were moving to a location with lower malpractice rates or retiring because of such suits.

A hospital in Reading, Pa. is unable to obtain malpractice coverage to cover state minimum coverage of $10 million but can obtain coverage above that minimum, thus creating a $10,000,000 deductible.

The cost of premiums for malpractice insurance for Stephen Barrar, Chief of Neurosurgery at Abington Hospital has risen from $70,000 in 2000 to $132,000 in 2001 to $314,000 in 2002. There are 20% fewer neurosurgeons in Pennsylvania than in 1998.

Throughout Pennsylvania, 20 mammography clinics closed their door in the past year due to a shortage of radiologists with training to read mammograms. Nationwide, only 4% of radiologists take such training because of the extremely high incidence of litigation, high cost of malpractice coverage and low reimbursements.

The severe shortage of radiologists specializing in reading mammograms has increased the wait time for screening mammograms at major hospitals to two or three months. One hospital reports a 14 to 16 week wait for mammograms to be screened. With the breast cancer "cure" being directly related to early diagnosis, waiting three months for a mammogram can make the difference between survival and death for a woman with a particular virulent strain of breast cancer.

Some Pennsylvania counties report a 100% increase in malpractice premiums from year 2001 to 2002. One county reported losing six doctors per month.

Although the Philadelphia Metropolitan Area may be the most litigation prone locale in the country, the rest of the areas can be sure that lawyers have the doctors in their sights as well.

States with very critical situations but forming a second tier somewhat below those three that were formerly mentioned are New

Jersey, New York, Ohio, Oregon, Florida, Washington, Texas, and West Virginia.

In two counties in Texas, in Charleston, West Virginia, and in one county of Mississippi, doctors have gone on strike to protest all of the lawsuits against doctors, most of them considered to be frivolous.

Doctor Jose Igna, a 47 year old psychiatrist was been quoted as saying:

"We're doctors. We train more than half of our lives to help people. We don't want to cause harm to anybody. We understand that when we cause damage, we want people to be fairly compensated. But when it comes to legal extortion, …it changes the way we practice medicine."

In another county, 63 per cent of doctors have had claims filed against them in the past 13 years. One physician expressed the common hope, "This is a plea for survival of doctors and patients."

Physicians and medical students are increasingly reluctant to practice in the crisis states. In the town of Bisbee, Arizona, the only hospital closed it's emergency ward, because family practitioners were seeing their rates rise to $88,000 per year.

California is one state that has met the problem head on with a law called the California Medical Injury Compensation Law which limits the amounts and compensation and has saved doctors of that state a billion dollars in liability premiums each year. A bill patterned after the California legislation has been submitted to Congress of the United States on the same basis called the Health (help efficiency, accessibility, low cost, timely, health care) Act of 2002"

As in every effort to place limits on litigation, the lobby which stands adamantly opposed is one that includes thousands of lawyers. The Association of Trial Lawyers of America includes 56,000 lawyers and, according to the Center for Responsible Politics, has already raised 1.5 million dollars to be spent during the current election cycle. That makes it the most powerful Political Action Committee in the nation.

In December, 2001, St. Paul Companies, the nation's second largest insurer against malpractice announced that it would no longer provide medical malpractice insurance. For the year 2001, it was going to have to pay out $1.99 in costs and damage payments on malpractice for each $1.00 that it received in premiums. No company could survive with such operating costs. This company had insured 42,000 doctors and 750 hospitals. When the current policies expire, doctors will pay 300% more for new coverage. That will mean as much as $400,000 for neurosurgeons and other hazardous specialties. Four other insurance companies are similarly dropping malpractice as a coverage.

My overwhelming impression after discussing the situation with doctors and surgeons is that they feel hemmed in by the threat of lawsuits with the pressure of potential accusations waiting their every move. They studied long years to prepare for the practice of medicine and instead, the ability to practice medicine in a professional atmosphere, they have the feeling that a vulture is waiting to strike. That more than anything takes the emphasis off of being able to help the patient who needs help and instead the thought must always be to wait the hounding assault from an aggressive lawyer. The proper word is merciless.

"Don't use my name," said more than one doctor after relevant information had been supplied, "because there are lawyers in this town that I may have to deal with." A genuine atmosphere of fear!

Sad it is to say that some doctors feel that <u>it is better to let a patient die than to attempt heroic surgery which might save the person's life</u>, <u>but where they might fail and be subject to a law suit.</u>

Chapter 12

Nightmare for the Pharmaceutical Innovators

The human body is not a finite structure subject to precise mathematical formulae. When an engineer or architect designs a 100 story steel building, a sufficient amount of testing has been done in laboratories so that the strength of steel is well established and the structure can be designed with precision.

With the human body, however, every one is different and subject to varying physiological patterns. Blood pressures will be different. The conditioning of muscles will exist at all variations. Concentrations of potassium will differ. And on and on.

Yet new diseases are continually developing in the swamps and in the equatorial rain forests. Vaccines must be developed. A continuing wide range of new drugs is needed to fight the oncoming diseases. New vaccines and drugs must be tested, first with laboratory animals but eventually with human guinea pigs.

One attorney, a representative of the drug developers, has described a typical biochemical company. It spends 800 million dollars on research over 10 years. From that work may come 5000 possible new drugs. In testing, five of those drugs may some day reach the stage of clinical testing and from the five, one will some day receive FDA approval.

The patent office requires the release of a great deal of advance disclosure as part of the patent procedure. Then come the lawyers!

Ah, yes, the lawyers! Almost never does a drug complete the process without at least one law suit for patent infringement. Legal costs on fighting such a suit may run $75,000 per day.

Yet, one of those gushers may come in and make the company millions of dollars of profit per day. One successful drug brought to market may turn a small corporation into a huge one. But one lost patent infringement suit may turn a large company into a small one.

There is even a more hazardous side to contacts between the pharmaceutical companies and lawyers because lawyers are quick to convince gullible, manipulable jurors that every test during the clinical testing period should turn out as a total success. If not, the lawyers sue. In reality, the failure probably means that the developmental process has moved beyond the state of the art. The lawyers still sue, and the jurors buy their arguments.

In any group of children who receive vaccinations, some will become ill. Was the vaccine the cause? Scientists at the Federal Drug Administration say that is very rare and so that arm of government had given approval to the drug. But to the lawyers, that doesn't matter. The lawyers can still sue the manufacturers. A persuasive tort lawyer just needs to persuade a jury and the company can be slapped with an enormous lawsuit.

The result is that the manufacturers decide that they are no longer going to innovate.

The tragedy is not the relatively few patients who succumb to the vaccination. The tragedy is for that great host of people who need an effective drug to overcome their health problem and a drug that might have been readily available with proper innovative effort that simply isn't in the works.

The matter of the breast implants by Dow Corning has been previously publicized but there have been other major attacks. 300,000 women claimed damages from the Dalkon shield with total settlements running to 2.6 billion dollars.

In lawsuits over diet drugs during the 1990s, settlements hit 13 billion dollars and reduced the ownership value of the company from $7 billion to $2.8 billion. Once again, too many of the public believe that takes from the rich when in reality, it hits millions of relatively small stockholders.

Lawsuits demand that 30 million babies born since 1990 be tested for autism on the theory that a preservative once used may have contained mercury. There is no scientific proof but if the lawyers can get that claim before juries, the damages may be done without scientific proof.

The most damming condition of all is that AIDS research is being reduced because of the fear of law suits. Imagine the impact on the economy of the United States if every death resulting from AIDS should be judged by benevolent juries to have been caused by attempted use of some hopeful drug remedy and failed. Further, imagine the horror if some wonder drug were withheld from testing because of fear of lawsuits when that drug might have saved thousands.

This is not a plea for the lawyers to take it easy on the corporations. It is a plea for them to allow the pharmaceutical innovators to develop the drugs that are needed for human beings and animals.

Chapter 13

Contrast between Assaults on Asbestos and Tobacco

Possibly no set of circumstances so totally illustrates the worthlessness of the punitive damages against corporations as the contrast of the results of the assaults on the asbestos and tobacco industries.

Asbestos has been in use since Roman times with historians of that era mentioning slaves working in the asbestos mines. The qualities that have made it so valuable are that it will not burn and that it transmits heat at almost an imperceptible rate. It was known as the "Miracle Mineral". The need for the material has been totally utilitarian with principal usages being home insulation, boiler insulation, floor tile, paint texturizing, automobile brakes and clutches, fireproofing, fire containment and ceiling panels.

It may well be true that if the steel structural members of the two World Trade Center had been fireproofed as normally done in industrial complexes, the two towers may never have collapsed and thousands of lives would have been saved. But at the time that the buildings were constructed, the use of asbestos was becoming a no-no.

In a sense, the entire campaign against asbestos has been a phantom battle based on the fact that jurors can be conned into believing that the material is a deadly danger.

Researchers were learning that asbestos could cause two forms of cancer, mesothelonia and asbestosis. The former involves deposits in the layer of tissue around the heart and lungs. A mitigating factor, however, was that mesothelonia occurs almost exclusively in patients with a history of smoking. So what part of a damage claim should be blamed on the presence of asbestos and what part on the cigarette industry. Maybe, more importantly, the disease does not show up until 20 years to 50 years after exposure to asbestos. That means that a great majority of the potential victims will die of other causes before the disease develops.

Current patterns are that about 30 cases of mesothelonia develop per year. As a comparison, we readily accept the number of deaths from vehicular accidents at around 41,000 each year as a normal result of the use of our highways. Many of the survivors from the highways are in near death or in pain inducing circumstances.

The potential for cancer provided the opportunity for the lawyers, and they had the advantage that two huge government bureaucracies, the Occupational Safety and Health Administration and the Environmental Protection Agency joined in the fight to eliminate the asbestos industry by means of the lawsuit.

The consulting firm, Tillinghast, Towers, and Perrin, estimates that the total amount of damages against the asbestos companies will eventually reach two hundred billion dollars. 33 corporations have been driven into bankruptcy. 85% of U.S. industry is now under attack for asbestos lawsuits. 90% of plaintiffs in those suits are not medically impaired.

Probably the largest single corporate assault was against Johns-Manville Company where the claims were so numerous that in a bankruptcy settlement, the company had agreed to pay off claims at 10 cents on the dollar. The claims kept pouring in and later the company had to reduce that to five cents on the dollar.

Asbestos claims have already cost the American economy more than the combined impact of the 9/11 destruction of the World Trade Towers, the Enron failure and the WorldCom failures combined. The U.S. Supreme Court has declared the asbestos morass unsolvable without help from the legislative branch.

In the course of business, The Dow Chemical Company acquired Union Carbide and, without the knowledge of the directors, the assets of the acquisition included an old asbestos mine. Before the claims from that mine were finished, it cost Dow 630 million dollars.

In a different settlement, four claimants in Mississippi were paid $150 million because "they didn't have the disease but might become sick". In yet another case, the U.S. Supreme Court will review a case where a jury awarded six plaintiffs $5.8 million who have claimed emotional suffering from the fear that they might get asbestos-related cancer in the future. One of those workers claimed he had worked around asbestos for three months in the 1950s.

The on-going shutdown of the asbestos industry would appear to confirm that the punitive damage awards work very well in destroying an industry that is harmful to some extent. The bulk of the money has gone to the lawyers.

And what of tobacco? Was it another utilitarian product whose use was intended entirely for the benefit of mankind?   Hardly. However, tobacco did once serve a very useful purpose. In the first decade of the life of our nation, there was a desperate need for cash to build an economy on which the nation could survive. Tobacco became one of America's early contributions to trade with Europe. As the thirteen original states struggled to gain a sound economic footing, tobacco was one cash crop that could be sold wherever the ships would carry it to accumulate dollars that the almost bankrupt new nation needed to survive.

On a different front far into the 20th century, doctors and researchers learned that tobacco, like asbestos, could cause cancer. The lawyers had found another "cash cow" but this time, no one seems to want the industry closed down.

The tobacco industry has advantages which the asbestos industry did not possess. First, in the case of asbestos, the end user was not normally the decision maker, a role filled by the architects, engineers and designers.   Those entities could not be targeted by endless advertising that would overwhelm good judgment. Secondly, the principal users in the case of asbestos had been relatively small sized corporations without effective lobbying power.   Wasn't there a government agency that could step in to aid in the fight against the tobacco industry as OSHA and the EPA had done in the battle against asbestos? Indeed, the Food and Drug Administration attempted to exercise their power of government to nullify the dangers which the Surgeon General had judged to be a cause of cancer. The Supreme Court of the United States ruled, however, that the FDA had no authority to exercise its power in behalf of the people of the United States.

In addition, the tobacco industry could generate a steady stream of new users at an age when those new smokers were making decisions based on teenage peer pressures rather than being concerned about their own long term mortality. When it came to the time in the jury room when the decisions were being made to grant large punitive awards, the jurors were ignoring the matter that the future victims had made their own decisions to become smokers.

Finally, the lawyers weren't required to prove scientifically that the tobacco was the cause of a cancer over which they were suing. They merely needed to convince a jury that such was the case and then persuade a gullible jury to award not only damage awards, but more importantly, punitive awards which would "teach the tobacco companies a lesson". Best of all, if they could find somewhere in the company files a report which confirmed that a company employee knew that the cigarettes could cause cancer, they could sell the jury on a massive award.

If ever there was proof that the lawyer's claim of eliminating problems by assessing huge punitive damages doesn't work, it was the tobacco industry. The corporation simply raised the price and created a greater evil.

This book has been very condemnatory of the endless lawsuits that have been unleashed against industry after industry. In those that we have described, society would have been better off if no lawsuit had ever been filed against any airplane manufacturer, the physicians and surgeons, or the prescription drug manufacturers.

For tobacco, however, where is the redeeming virtue? What property serves humanity that can justify the continuing production of such a health threat? Surely we must accept the findings of doctors and researchers. How many lives have been laid waste by that evil among men?

I will not belabor the argument that tobacco is an island of seemingly total evil in the economic mix of America. The reader will remember than I am highly approving of the corporation as a key tool of our economic system. And indeed the corporations were striving to satisfy the need for pleasure filled relaxation when the tobacco corporations were founded. That was before we knew how many would die from exposure to those restful pauses.

Let me merely review the curse of advertising as it contributes to the habits that we can't seem to exterminate. Even if we were to concur, however, that tobacco yields a totally negative impact, we do not know how to dismantle that industry. Too many economic interests are involved – the farmers who grow the tobacco– the tobacco processing plants – the cigarette makers – the corporations who market the product – the trucking industry – the stockholders who own the company and prosper from the earnings - and the advertisers. Ah yes, the advertisers.

In 1998, a settlement with many states provided a staggering amount of money from the tobacco industry One of the stipulations of that agreement was that those companies would minimize the advertising in the situations where smoking would appeal to minors. Yet two years after that agreement, the tobacco companies were, according to the Federal Trade Commission, spending 42% of total revenues on advertising. That's $26 million dollars per day to advertise cigarettes with most of the money going into promotions that will appeal to teenagers. Studies have shown that the heaviest concentration of placards that advertise cigarettes is in convenience stories. Other studies disclose that 75% of teenagers shop in convenience stores on the way to or from school.

A common place for advertising has been in the magazines that would attract the attention of teenagers such as Sports Illustrated and Rolling Stones Magazine. Likewise, promotional events such as the Virginia Slims Tennis Tournament and the Winston Marlboro Speedway races are advertised on the boxes of cereal that the teenager's mother places in front of them. Or when their parent takes them to the doctor's offices, they find the magazines with the unacceptable advertising. Or if a parent takes them to a baseball game in a minor league park, the most prevalent advertising on the outfield fences is that of cigarettes. Not targeting youth?

I now have in front of me a recorded tape of western music titled "The Best of Marlboro Country Music" with such artists as Merle Haggard, George Strait, Alabama, The Judds, and Randy Travis. It is an old one but still a reflection of our life style.

Not long ago, the nation's courts were carrying on a crusade to punish the tobacco companies for the long time sale of tobacco. North Carolina's share of that giant lawsuit was $5.6 billion dollars. And what does a state do with it's receipts from such a sum of money? 3/4 of that money has gone back into promoting the industry. That state chose to pay 50 million dollars to tobacco growers to modernize their equipment so they could grow more tobacco. The politicians are the biggest problem of all.

In the most recent lawsuit in behalf of a tobacco user, the jury awarded punitive damages of $28 billion. That is one jury that, even though irrational, was trying to dismantle the tobacco industry but the judge reduced the amount to $28 million.

With the continuing growth of cigarette sales in the United States, it is clear that punitive awards have meant nothing.

Chapter 14

The Illogical World of Law

No circumstances so well illuminate the lack of firmly based logic in the legal profession than two cases which resulted from drivers who committed traffic offenses.

Domino's Pizza developed a marketing program to fight the competitive battle for customers by publicizing a policy that any pizza would be delivered to the door of the person ordering the pizza within 30 minutes. If the customer was not satisfied either with the time of delivery or the quality of the pizza, the company would refund the full price of the pizza or replace it. This campaign moved Domino into the high ranks of pizza sales.

To augment that policy, each franchise recruited a crew of drivers who were driving a total of two million miles a day to deliver pizza on time

With that many drivers on the road, Domino's Pizza felt it necessary to develop a safety program to protect both the drivers and the public. Their safety program had four facets.

a. Before any applicant was considered for hire, the company ran a motor vehicle check to ensure a two year safe driving record.
b. Once hired, each driver was required to complete safety and training programs.

c. The company's safety education program won a special public service award from the U.S. Department of Transportation in 1993.
d. The company issued a Driver Training Video that won an award for safety in corporate communications.

For 14 years, the company used the program at 5300 locations with what they judged to be great success. The quick availability of Pizza became part of the American culture.

In spite of the safety efforts of the company, however, one of the company's drivers was involved in an accident in which Jean Kinder was seriously injured but not killed. A jury ordered Domino's Pizza to pay the woman $750,000 in actual damages and $78 million dollars in punitive damages.

The matter of the award for punitive action was discussed in Chapter 7 but the lawsuit left the woman and the lawyers with a healthy bank account. Now let's look at a different traffic violation.

In Colorado, Ike Lucero ran a stop sign and collided with a mini-van carrying eight members of a California family. Four of the eight died from the crash and Lucero was charged with vehicular homicide.

Officers of the Colorado State Patrol estimated that Lucero was traveling at 80 miles per hour when he went through the stop sign but a defense "expert" estimated his speed at 35 miles per hour. A significant difference!

The judge informed the jury that the mere occurrence of an accident did not imply negligence by the driver of the van and the jury reacted by finding Lucero innocent of all charges except for 8 counts of failure to yield the right-of-way, one count for each of the dead and injured. The total punishment was a fine of $100!

The defense attorney had placed blame largely on the design and maintenance of the highway intersection. One failure to stop at a stop light with no deaths caused a penalty $54,000,000. Another failure to stop with four deaths caused a penalty of $100. The lawyers made fools of the jurors.

In a New York City subway station, Bernard McCummings was looking for a score and he and his three companions had an idea on how to get a few dollars. They mugged and partially choked a prosperous looking Jerome Sandusky but that resulted in only a $30 haul. Fortunately, his cries for help came to the attention of two New York City police officers. In the melee that followed while the police were attempting to place the three men in custody, McCummings was shot with a shattering of the spine, thus creating paralysis below the waist.

Rules had been newly issued that said that guns would only be used as defensive weapons. They were not to be used to stop a fleeing felon "unless there is probable cause to believe that the felon will use deadly force"...There was no question that the policeman's life was threatened but in the excitement of the battle, that officer acted instinctively without remembering the new rules of the game.

McCummings had just departed prison after a two year term for a robbery conviction. If the shots had not brought him down, he would have been out on the streets to attack still more victims and almost certain to kill someone sooner or later because in the mugging, this victim had very nearly been killed.

The felon sued and received a jury award of $4.3 million dollars. Part of the reason for the large settlement according to jury members, was that McCummings was now deprived of any future sex life.

In another situation, when Mary Salazar was given an injection in her left buttock, some of the tissue died and she was left with an indented scar. The jury ordered the hospital to pay her $18,000 for that disfiguring scar.

In another episode, police were pursuing an automobile in a high speed chase. The felons crossed a jurisdictional boundary and were eventually stopped by a policeman in the new jurisdiction. The court released the accused because the arresting policeman had no certain knowledge of the original crime. He only knew that the fleeing felon was wanted by police.

Revered and now deceased writer Mike Royko related the episode where Ernie Mota was arrested for driving while intoxicated in the Chicago suburb of Oak Park. Mota was an illegal immigrant from Mexico and had a history of many arrests for armed robbery, kidnapping, drunken driving and drug peddling.

At the police station, he was searched and was asked what he had in his pocket. As he turned his pockets inside out, a plastic bag fell to the floor that would be revealed to have been filled with cocaine. To avoid having the cocaine seized as evidence, Mota tried to swallow it. As soon as the police realized what he was doing, they tried to stop him but he managed to swallow a good portion of the powdered substance.

Mota was placed in a cell where he suffered some of the effects that might have been expected. The town's doctor was called to treat him and was barely able to save his life. His brain was damaged by the heavy dose of cocaine and he may have suffered some loss of vision.

Ernie's lawyer sued the town of Oak Forest and the four police officers who had handled Mota at the police station. The claim was that the city had not been sufficiently trained its police and that they had not recognized the emergency soon enough. They should have called the doctors more promptly. They asked for seven million dollars for the criminal and his lawyer.

In Sapulpa, Oklahoma, Judge April Sellers White sentenced John Marquez to life imprisonment for spitting on Officer Charles Gadd. The judge could have opted for a shorter sentence of 25 years in prison but the jury had recommended a maximum sentence. The rationale for the apparently stiff sentence was that the law had been enacted when the AIDs crusade was it's greatest leading to a law against placing bodily fluids on law enforcement officers. Marquez tested negative for any communicable disease. An appeal is pending.

Thomas Grasso first killed a citizen of New York and was convicted with a sentence to serve 20 years. He escaped and moved to Oklahoma. There he killed again and was once again convicted. This time he was given a death penalty, but New York Governor Mario Cuomo insisted and a judge ruled that he must be returned to New York to complete his sentence in that state, where he could be available to be tried again for the escape before being executed in Oklahoma.

Then he would have been able to begin the appeals process which might have lasted for another 20 years. Fortunately, a new Governor, George Pitacki, had made the Grasso case an election issue and when he was inaugurated in New York, he agreed to allow Grasso's request that he be transferred to the death row of the Oklahoma prison at

McAlester. That action also saved the State of New York at least half a million dollars that it would have cost to house and feed him at Attica prison for 20 years.

Mr. Peacock was a long distance truck driver who was detoured from part of his scheduled route because of a serious snow storm. He cut short his trip to arrive at home and find his wife in bed with another man. Instead of resolving the problem at that time, he went to a bar and spent the afternoon soothing his feelings with alcohol. Finally, he went home and shot his wife who was then alone.

Mr. Peacock was sentenced to eighteen months in prison plus fifty hours of community service for killing his wife.

Edward Bello, 60, had a long string of arrests and conviction but had never spent a day in prison. In 2001, he plead guilty to use of a stolen credit card. The judge sentenced him to 10 months in detention and specified that he was not to be allowed to watch television.

The judge added:

> "It is thus important that the normal diversion of television watching be denied, in order that he may have ample opportunity to reflect on the ways of harm that he has brought to his family."

The United States Court of Appeals stayed the sentence on the basis that he had been denied his rights under the First Amendment.

There will be those readers who will detect that many of the examples in this book are from the 1960s. This is because the Warren Court of the 1950s announced numerous ground breaking decisions and it took only a few years before major impacts evolved. Rules to implement the guidelines tended to come in the 60s. Lawyers who write books commonly illustrate their points with cases from the sixties.

We must not forget one more case. Juan Corona is a famous mass murderer who was convicted of hacking 25 transient farm workers to death with a machete and burying them in orchards around the Yuba River Valley of California. When the judge learned that the defense attorney was taking notes to prepare information for a new book, he declared the trial contaminated and ordered a totally new trial.

Later in that same case, the appeals court once again ordered a new trial because his attorneys had failed to offer a defense of temporary insanity.

Chapter 15

An Undersized but Revealing Sample

Motivation for this book did not originate from my own experiences with lawyers but the contacts certainly didn't calm my concerns. If we review the history of every instance when I have gone to lawyers during my 60 years of adult life with an expectation to pay for the lawyer's services, it is a sorry record.

Admittedly, a sample of 16 contacts in 60 years out of the millions of attorney-client contacts in the United States is an infinitely small sample but the results may be a better statement of the effectiveness of lawyers than they would care to admit.

Let's save the reader from wading through the boring details of the insignificant episodes and simply indicate that four successful ventures were accomplished from the 16 engagements. They included a simple will, review of a prenuptial agreement, action to protect property against a potential claim resulting from a bankruptcy action by another person, and an opening conference for a divorce that was under consideration.

The unsatisfactory contacts among that group of 10 minor actions involved flawed legal actions, excessive fees, unprofessional conduct, incorrect advice (twice), excessive delay before beginning a task, endless requests to cover costs for a patent search, and disappearance of attorneys (twice) without completing the intended tasks. Those last two were after accepting a combined $1042 in partial fees (I am not suggesting that these were improper charges but rather accumulated charges on work that they would never complete through no fault of mine). One attorney moved back to New York and in the other case, the attorney encountered ill health and terminated practice without arranging for anyone to take over the practice.

Two incidents were substantial violations of any code of ethics. In one episode, while I was operating a ServiceMaster Cleaning Service, the manager of a real estate management company called me and asked that our company clean an apartment which the previous tenant, a young unmarried lady, had left in a state of unconscionable filth.

The manager simply said, "Go clean the place, paint the walls, and send us the bill. We are going to take that young lady to court to collect for the cleaning work."

When I examined the apartment, there was much work to be done. The one task that concerned me most was the electric oven. I had never seen such a dirty, encrusted oven.

The principle component of oven cleaner is sodium hydroxide, commonly known to most housewives as lye. With the damage that lye could cause, particularly skin damage or blindness, I chose never to expose any of my employees to such a risk. I knew that, even though business owners do not normally do such work, I would wear proper protective wear so I always did serious oven cleaning myself.

The baked-on remains of food were built up to near 1/8th inch in thickness over the entire oven. (This was not a self-cleaning oven) I worked one Saturday morning from eight until noon before it was finally in a usable condition once again.

I was paid for the work and the first time I saw the young lady who had created the filth was from the witness stand. I testified truthfully on the entire billing costs and, since I had done the work personally, I was able to give a graphic description of the condition of the oven.

The judge rendered his verdict in favor of the young lady. He justified the verdict on the basis that he had often watched his wife clean the oven in their kitchen and he knew that it did not take more than fifteen minutes. His judgment was that if I had exaggerated the work on every part of the cleaning effort as much as I had exaggerated the work on the oven, then there was no case against the young lady.

We later learned that the young lady was soon to be married to the son of a fellow judge on the municipal bench.

On the final case, I will abstain from using the name of the attorney not because there is any untruth in my version but because it illustrates one of the flaws in the relationship between attorneys and clients. If the lawyer should sue me for defamation of character, he could obtain legal services at little cost. He could cause me to have to hire a competent attorney and although I was confident that I would surely win in any trial before a jury, the attorney fees for my defense would be his revenge against me.

When my mother, a resident of Chickasha, Oklahoma, died in 1991, my brother and I were her only living heirs. It seemed logical that we would go to the lawyer whose firm had served our family for eight decades.

She had owned various stocks and bonds which, on advice of her stock broker, had been placed in a Transfer on Death (TOD) Account. Having been created under the laws of the state of Missouri, this procedure, later utilized by other states as the Payable on Death Account, was relatively new as one of those legal devices that allow a person to eliminate their assets from probate. This pattern had been approved by the Internal Revenue Service for use in every state in the union.

When my mother died on December 6, 1991, my brother and I decided on an initial action of a brief visit to her stockbroker. We inquired on the procedure to transfer over a hundred thousand dollars in TOD investments to us as beneficiaries. We were informed that we needed a tax waiver certificate from the Oklahoma Tax Commission. In most cases of which the broker was aware, the beneficiaries handled that effort themselves. However, since we both lived out of state, and handling it would have meant trips to the tax office in Oklahoma City, he recommended that we use the services of a Certified Public Accountant. To his best knowledge, that normally cost $200 to $300. That amount was later confirmed by a CPA.

An alternative course would be to request the certificate through the attorney who had drawn up and would probate my mother's will.

The broker also informed us that it should take 10 to 14 days to obtain the needed certificate. Once the tax waiver certificate was in hand, his brokerage company would handle all further activities to transfer the assets to us without charge.

A couple of days after her funeral, we made a visit to the attorney. My mother's will named me as her Personal Representative and I delivered a copy of the safety deposit box inventory. I wanted to establish the fee in advance.

The attorney stated that the fee would be "$1000 to $1100, maybe $1,150". Although there was no need to mention it, I believed I should have no secrets from my attorney so I told him about the TOD account with the brokerage firm and said that I was going to have a CPA start the process of getting the tax waiver certificates. The attorney interrupted me to say, "Oh, I'll get that for you for nothing. There isn't much effort to that." Later in the meeting, he repeated a second time that as long as he was not going to be involved in the transfer of the stocks and bonds, he would get the tax waiver certificate at no charge to the estate.

I told him that the broker had indicated the certificate should be obtainable within 14 days. Did he have any problem with that?

He replied that there should be no difficulty. I should have gone home, borrowed a typewriter and typed up a statement summarizing the proposed fee, describing the offer to get the tax waiver certificate for nothing, and then added that the certificate was expected to be obtained in 14 days. Then I should have taken my statement back to the attorney for signature. But aren't you supposed to be able to trust your attorney?

My brother and I then agreed that we would act in reliance on his offer and allow him to obtain the certificate for us. As soon as that certificate had been obtained, the stock broker would proceed with the process of transferring the stocks and bonds.

The second stage for the attorney was the forgetting process.

Over the ensuing weeks, my brother and I had a total of eight long distance telephone conversations with the Chickasha lawyer where we were pushing for speedy action on the TOD account for which he had agreed to obtain the tax certificate within 14 days. During this period he was becoming more and more vague about the TOD account and my brother needed to have the matter settled. Finally, four months after the first agreement, he called the Oklahoma lawyer and the following conversation ensued (as my brother remembered it).

My brother asked, "Has any progress been made on the tax waiver certificate?"

"What tax waiver certificate?"

"The one for the TOD account."

"She didn't have any TOD account."

"Oh, yes, she did, with the XYZ brokerage company." Then when my brother started to explain, the attorney said,

"Oh yes, now I guess I remember."

My brother had come to believe that the lawyer was maneuvering to charge a much larger fee than agreed and to treat the assets in the TOD account as if they were part of the probated assets. I, as personal representative, should have stopped everything right there and discharged him as our attorney.

After one more call by my brother, I personally called the lawyer and asked about the tax waiver certificate. He seemed to be completely puzzled. His answer to me was, "I guess I am going to have to go see the broker to see what that TOD account is all about."

Finally, 4½ months after agreeing to obtain the tax waiver certificate in two weeks at no charge, he had shifted the circumstances by a process of forgetting or pretending to forget.

I received a letter from the lawyer that I would later come to comprehend better because he was telling me that he was going to have to base his fee on the total assets of the estate including the TOD account rather than on the total of probate estate as provided by the fee schedule for Oklahoma lawyers. There was no mention of how much fee might have been contemplated.

On May 26, I had an extended telephone conversation with the supervisor of the Oklahoma Tax Commission who should have been involved in the case and finally received a full explanation on what could have been done by the lawyer to provide a quick release of the tax waiver certificate back in December and what must now be done to expedite it. But he stated that nothing had been done yet. His summary was that the state tax office had not even opened a file on my mother's estate because there had been no communication of any kind from the attorney.

Meanwhile, sale of our mother's home was totally stalled. We had found a buyer during those first days after her death, provided a signed contract and turned to the lawyer to handle the legal steps since, while the stocks and bonds were not part of the estate under probate, the house was.

Finally on two days in late May, I made five telephone calls to the lawyer and to the escrow company. Each was blaming the other for the standstill. Finally, after the final call, I persuaded them to talk to one another on the telephone. The sale of the house was completed within four days.

The groundwork had been somehow laid to demand a larger fee. A statement of the higher fee must be presented to the Personal Representative, namely, me.

In early June, an action occurred which was the first step toward obtaining the long sought tax waiver certificate. But it was also time for the lawyer to try to slip a haymaker past my upraised guard. I received an estate tax report from the lawyer that, according to the cover memo, only needed my signature and it could be returned to him to initiate the formal process that would release the tax waiver certificate.

I suspected that somewhere in the five pages of the report, I would find the fee that he intended to charge us. It showed up on page 4 with no mention in the cover letter. The tax report called for not $1000 to $1150 of fees as agreed but for a total of $4260. That represented $2760 related to the TOD account and which was therefore being substituted for the zero fee that he had offered earlier. There were other blatant errors in the balance of this report so I returned the tax report and agreed to sign a corrected version when I visited his office later that month. A corrected version would mean with no fee for the TOD account.

When I subsequently visited his office he totally refused to discuss his estimate of fee of $1000 to $1150 or the December agreement to obtain the tax waiver certificate for nothing. His only reaction was that since he and I were not in agreement on a fee, we would go to a hearing in district court and allow the judge to establish the fee. He totally refused to discuss anything that might have been discussed at the December meeting.

A final hearing was eventually held as my brother and I went with him before District Judge Oteka L. Alford. She showed no interest at all about our description of the initial agreement that had occurred on December 10, nor in the meaning or legal impact of the Transfer on Death Account. Instead, she apparently attempted to strike an approximate middle ground between the $4260 which he had demanded and the approximate $1100 which had been agreed. The total fee was assigned by the judge was $2943, far above the "$1000 to $1100, maybe $1150" that had been agreed. There was no indication of how much of the judge's determination of fee was related to the TOD account but obviously it was about $1850.

If I had never mentioned the TOD account in the lawyer's office, we would have also had no need for thousands or dollars in expenses that it cost us to make trips to Oklahoma to settle the problems

When I telephoned the Oklahoma Bar Association to discuss the conduct of this miscreant, I was also informed that in a small town like Chickasha, I would find no attorney willing to pursue action against a local attorney. They operated in the same court system. All attorneys in a small town know that they must deal with each other on a daily basis and they and the judge were unwilling to stir hostility between the practitioners.

Those four previously mentioned successes in 16 episodes may be closer to a representative sampling of the competency, quality of performance and integrity of attorneys in the United States than we would hope.

Chapter 16

Defense Attorneys - - - and Prosecuting Attorneys

The Defenders

In August, 2002, David Westerfield was convicted of murdering 7 year old Danielle Van Damm and the nation waited for almost two weeks before the jury decided to recommend a punishment of death by lethal injection. Then came a bombshell story. The two lawyers for Westerfield had known that he had murdered the child and, in the period immediately before her body had been found, they were trying to plea bargain an agreement whereby they would take officials to the child's body in exchange for an agreement that he would be spared from the death penalty.

During the crucial part of the trial, the defense lawyers, Robert Boyce and Steven Feldman, concocted a tale of a pattern of events whereby the murdered girl's parents lived a somewhat unsavory lifestyle and they tried to sell the jury on the idea that child molesters had attended their parties. One of them had to have been the likely killer.

A San Diego newspaper revealed the secret negotiations over the attempted plea bargain and talk show hosts were outraged. They were certain that, by having full knowledge of their clients guilt and yet offering a defense to the contrary, the two attorneys had violated the California Code of Ethics and they sought a complaint with the California Bar Association.

As a guest on one program, William Nimmo, a San Diego criminal defense attorney, informed the host that defense attorneys would have been in violation of the constitution if they had failed to do all possible to defend their client, even to presenting false testimony. He repeatedly referred to the 1971 case of United States v. Wade.

The conditions where Nimmo was supported was that while there was no such wording in the Constitution itself, there had been a Supreme Court decision that had interpreted the Constitution to mean exactly that. Unfortunately, that is a circumstance that exists for all too many of the actions which the defense chooses to take to defend their clients.

The catch-all policy that makes every defense to be considered justified, is the long standing summation that, as a trained lawyer, the defense attorney has the proper knowledge and access to the full spectrum of law and legal actions that can be used to defend the client. That being so, it is the lawyer's responsibility to use that knowledge to take every course of action that the defendant would exercise if he had the same skill and knowledge. Assuredly, a murderer in danger of the death penalty, would have no hesitation to present evidence that he knows to be false. And the lawyer should do the same, per the ruling dicta.

We have previously revealed the "Three Hardest Questions" whereby an ethics professor has opened the door for a defense lawyer to impeach an adverse witness who is known to be telling the truth, to present a witness when it is known that he or she will commit perjury, or give his client legal advice when he believes that the knowledge will tempt him to commit perjury.

The answer that the legal expert provided for all of these questions was the affirmative. Those answers further opened the door for a defense attorney to do as Boyce and Feldman did.

The law books are filled with hundreds, no, thousands, of uncertain rules that have grown out of court decisions at every level. The proliferation of legal rulings or rules has been something like the development of the computer. The first computer was a relatively simple thing, one that could be built with a number of on-off switches. Daily, even hourly, someone thought of a new use for some improvement and the computer became more complex. Today the computer is a machine of incredible complexity. Similarly, in the beginning, legal doctrine was relatively simple. Some lawyer thought of a concept that was not necessarily better but which served the cause which he was arguing. The courts that reviewed that concept reasoned that it wasn't too far from some rule that was already in effect and so the court approved the concept as being similar to the words that were already in effect.

The fifth amendment's "No person...shall be compelled in any criminal case to be a witness against himself" was extended to mean that "a wife cannot be compelled to testify against her husband"; "the accused's past criminal record cannot be used against him "and "a doctor-patient relationship is privileged". All were represented to be a form of testifying against oneself and thus were said to be forbidden by the constitution.

A reasonable person can conceive of situations where mental coercion can justifiably be termed to be compulsion within the meaning of the fifth amendment. Yet I believe that level of being manipulated would have to be something equivalent to mental torture. Certainly, if a person's infant child was being threatened with harm, that would compel any reasonable parent to yield to the pressure. The Supreme Court, however, has taken the meaning of mental coercion or mental compulsion to unbelievable extremes which I believe far exceed the meaning of the original amendment.

There is no way, for example, that "tweaking a person's conscience" could constitute compulsion but it is part of the repertoire of the defense attorney. Somehow, a reasonable definition of the word "compulsion" is needed. That definition should be based on what a reasonable person would consider to be compulsion to which they would have to yield. In the physical sense, for example, no one should consider a pinch on the buttocks, as is often used as an inducement to manipulate small children, to be a reasonable form of physical compulsion but the range of decisions by the Supreme Court have accepted the mental equivalent of the pinch.

Most of us have at one time or another played the game where a large group of people are seated in a circle and the leader of the group relates a simple story to the person on his or her right and then that person repeats the story to the person to the right, and on the story goes around the circle. Each person unintentionally changes the meaning by an insignificant amount but by the time it arrives back at the starting point, the story has changed to the point that it is almost unrecognizable.

Just so, a principle evolves as it passes from one case to the next and with each new version, a new rule is formed that becomes part of the legal doctrine on which future appeals will be decided. It is the application of these manifold rules that cause lay people to declare that some accused person was freed because of a loophole. Today's new interpretation is tomorrow's loophole. That interpretation often seems unethical.

Combine those new interpretations with imaginative interpretations by the Supreme Court and appellate court justices who desire to accomplish a political agenda and the law books are equipped with an endless variety of loopholes.

In 1961, the United States Supreme Court issued what was to become known as the Exclusionary Rule that declared that any evidence obtained illegally must be excluded from evidence. The Supreme Court merely stated the philosophy and then left it to future decisions to determine precisely what that philosophy meant in terms of actual applications.

Unfortunately there has been a hailstorm of decisions which sum up to contradictory guidelines. Today, no police officer or judge can decide at the time that they act on what they believe to be one of the rules whether that action will be sustained by the judges.

We hear much criticism of judges in today's dialogue. What most of the public doesn't understand is that the judges do not know at the time that they are making a ruling whether that ruling will survive the inconsistency of future appellate decisions. Judges do not want to have their decisions thrown out.

Dominic Dunne, noted writer of crime stories, largely for Vanity Fair Magazine, relates the detailed events of trials of the wealthy and famous. He has written of the Menendez brothers trials, the O.J.

Simpson trial, the trial of Claus von Bulow and the like. Then came the day when his own daughter was brutally murdered in Beverly Hills. As the trial progressed, Dunne was horrified that the judge, Los Angeles Criminal Court Judge Burton S. Katz, the same judge who is sometimes quoted elsewhere in this book, ruled that testimony of the prolonged strangulation of Dunne's daughter was inadmissible. What Dunne apparently didn't know was that only a short time previously, the California Supreme Court, notorious for expanding the rights of the accused, had ruled that in an earlier trial of the same accused, John Sweeney, that the judge had improperly admitted evidence that a woman victim had been beaten to death by Sweeney. Relying on that preceding case, Katz was certain that the evidence of Sweeney having strangled Dominique Dunne would cause the trial verdict to be similarly thrown out so, using the previous trial as a guide, he ruled that evidence inadmissible. The jury ruled the death to be manslaughter and Katz was infuriated that his own ruling had misled the jury.

Those endless rules largely provide the defense lawyers with what most of the lay people angrily declare to be loopholes, for they defy what most people would call common sense. In any case they provide the opportunities to allow unnumbered accused to go free. Let's list just a few examples which have provided such opportunities.

1) Two officers walk up to a person standing near the trunk of a car and the man spontaneously volunteers information to the police that there is a body in the trunk of the car. The trunk is searched and sure enough, a body is found. The appeals court ruled that the confession was inadmissible because the man was intimidated by the presence of the officers.

2) Two jurors questioned whether a man could walk as far as he had testified in the stated period of time. They performed their own informal test to see if that statement was reasonable. Consequently, a conviction was overturned because they were making a decision of guilt or innocence based on something other than evidence that had been presented at the trial.

3) A woman carried a legal dictionary into the jury room and caused a trial to be terminated.

113

We could go on and on for thousands of rules that the attorneys and police officers are supposed to remember or cause to be followed. Too much evidence is rejected under what is called the Exclusionary rule. Attorneys literally form their reputations by either recalling some such rule and applying it at a crucial time or they originate their own new rule and apply to the appeals court to get that rule approved into long lasting legal doctrine.

Rules are so written that often what the police officer is thinking governs the determination of whether a search warrant is valid. The officers who went over the fence and searched the Rockingham estate of O.J. Simpson were an example. If the officers who made that decision had begun to believe that Simpson was the murderer and wanted to locate all possible evidence at his home, then the search was invalid and the judge should have refused to allow the evidence to be entered. However, if that decision maker believed that the trail of blood drops meant that there might be some injured person inside the estate who needed medical help and, while they were in the compound to give aid to that person, evidence was discovered, then the search warrant was not needed and admission of evidence was acceptable.

There are the endless rules that the police officers and judges are supposed to apply, some of them being distinctions that haven't yet been made. And the definitions are changing every day. It is impossible to develop a complete list of rules that the officer should follow, but there are instead general policies where appellate judges can proclaim a new interpretation with every new usage.

As another uncertainty, no one has been willing to permanently define a totally understandable meaning of "beyond a reasonable doubt". Yet jurors are told that they must decide that an accused is guilty beyond a reasonable doubt before declaring him or her to be guilty. That means that every juror has to develop his own idea of what that term means.

If one were to ask a lawyer what aspect of the conduct is law at it's finest, the reply well might be the fact that a lawyer can be trusted to keep information confidential. The American Bar Association's Model Rules of Professional Conduct prohibit lawyers from revealing confidential information except in limited circumstances. The general rule is that disclosure can occur only where necessary to prevent future criminal acts or criminal conduct that would result in imminent death or substantial bodily harm. However, some attorneys have maintained silence even to the point of causing great injustices.

The most notorious overdose of confidentiality occurred when, in 1915, an attorney heard his client confess to a murder for which a different man, Leo Frank, had been convicted and incarcerated. The attorney contacted the governor and informed him that Frank was innocent but would provide no information as to the source or reliability of the information. The governor commuted Frank's sentence but did not have sufficient information to grant a new trial. Leo Frank was hanged by a lynch mob. 70 years later, Frank was pardoned posthumously.

Later, the lawyer said, "I would be strongly tempted to break my oath before I would let an innocent man hang, but I would know that I was violating the law and my oath if I did so".

In another case, a man wrongly convicted of murder was allowed to sit on death row for 12 years while the attorney for the guilty man remained silent and advised his client, who had committed perjury, against confessing to the crime.

If clients refuse to take appropriate corrective action, an attorney's only recourse is to withdraw from representation and to disavow any of his own prior statements to third parties that might have assisted criminal or fraudulent conduct.

The state codes have given lawyers discretion to reveal confidential information only when necessary to defend themselves against accusations of their own wrongful conduct or to collect their fees.

The Prosecutors

I, as with most other observers of legal practice, was ready to believe that essentially all of the evil that occurred was part of the scheming by defense attorneys to cause a guilty man to go free. As I have studied a variety of texts, however, I have learned that the guilt by prosecutors is equally serious, particularly in the instance of ambitious prosecutors who want to advance their careers.

In 1940, Supreme Court Justice Robert Jackson said that the most dangerous power of a prosecutor is:

"...he will pick people that he thinks he should get rather than pick cases that need to be prosecuted.

"A prosecutor stands a fair chance of finding at least a technical violation of some act on the part of almost anyone. It is a question of picking the man and then searching the law books, or putting investigators to work, to pin some offense on him. It is in this realm – in which the prosecutor picks some person whom he dislikes or desires to embarrass - or selects some group of unpopular persons - and then looks for an offense, that the greatest danger of abuse from the prosecution lies. It is here that law enforcement becomes personal, and the real crime is that of being unpopular with the predominant or governing group, being attached to the wrong political views or being personally obnoxious to, or in the way of the prosecutor himself."

"Any prosecutor who risks his day-to-day professional name for fair dealing to build up statistics of success has a perverted sense of practical values, as well as defects of character...A sensitiveness to fair play and sportsmanship is perhaps the best protection against the abuse of power, and the citizen's safety lies in the prosecutor who tempers zeal with human kindness, who seeks truth and not victims, who serves the law and not factional purposes, and who approaches his task with humility."

Supreme Court Justice George Sutherland said essentially the same thing in 1934:

"The United States Attorney is the representative of a sovereignty whose interest in criminal prosecution is not that it shall win a case but that justice shall be done. As such...his twofold aim is that guilt shall not escape or innocence suffer. He may prosecute with earnestness and vigor...but while he may strike hard blows, he is not at liberty to strike foul ones.

It is as much his duty to refrain from improper methods calculated to produce a wrongful conviction as it is to use every legitimate means to bring about a just one."

Those are good statements of how the District Attorney should conduct his office. The general pattern of events, however, is that the office of U.S. District Attorney offers the most accessible path to ambitious lawyers who aspire to higher office, especially, congress or mayor. To achieve such goals, the District Attorney needs a record with a high percentage of convictions. With that in mind he announces that he will clean up the city. An unprincipled DA can select vulnerable targets, preferably someone who is not too popular in the community or with the press. The district attorney may release rumors to people who can be expected to reveal that information to some investigative reporter. The media then reveals that it has learned that charges are expected to be filed against the target suspect.

Next, the prosecuting attorney needs a witness who will testify before a grand jury. A likely choice is an accountant who has encountered legal trouble of his own and can be plea bargained into dropping charges in exchange for testifying, truthfully or falsely, against the chosen target. An even more likely choice is the undercover person who will join an organization to acquire information that will serve the purposes of the District Attorney. Another option is to place a prisoner in a cell with an intended target. By whatever method, the district attorney gets the witness that he needs, presses a conviction against the target person, and gains prominence for an upcoming race for public office. The prosecutors can collect more applicable evidence during the process of discovery, and soon will have the conviction to increase the percentage of successes.

Obviously, such a pattern does not develop in every case or even in a majority of cases, yet there are many critics of prosecutorial behavior who contend that it happens all too often. In fact, a law school textbook, Prosecutorial Misconduct by Bennett Gershman, a former prosecutor, is now in its second printing.

J. Edgar Hoover was named to the position of the Director of the Federal Bureau of Investigation at the age of 29, and he was determined to enforce rules that fully complied with the constitution. Serious legal objections had appeared criticizing the use of undercover informants because they could become yet another version of secret police which had been prevalent in such countries as Russia and Spain. Hoover advised the Attorney General against using the FBI to investigate communist activities in the United States because, "the Bureau would undoubtedly be subject to charges in the matter of alleged secret and undesirable methods". Later he objected to infiltrating the Vietnam war protest groups.

William C. Sullivan admitted in his memoirs that he had ignored Hoover's orders:

> "Some agents, especially the younger ones, infiltrated many of the groups in spite of Hoover's insisting to me that no agent should wear long hair, dress in jeans or wear scruffy clothes."

He wrote that Hoover also objected strongly to investigating crimes before they had occurred by having agents go undercover and incite people to commit crimes.

The shift away from a policy of prosecutors publicly adhering to constitutional patterns began in earnest during the Kennedy administration when the president's brother Robert, as attorney general, announced that he would pick the target, this time Jimmy Hoffa, and then search for crimes with which he could be charged. Kennedy's practice of bringing the full power of the U.S. government against a citizen quickly became a common practice.

After J. Edgar Hoover died, the pattern would begin a spiral when, in 1976, the FBI openly requested funds for undercover operations in the war against crime. Undercover policies were written into federal regulations during the Reagan administration and in the ensuing years, corruption in law enforcement would escalate.

In 1998, Congressman Joseph McDade, (R–Pennsylvania) would say,

> "There are Justice Department employees who engage in questionable conduct without penalty and without oversight,

using the full weight and power of the U.S. government. A win-at-all-costs attitude blinds them into suppressing exculpatory evidence, falsifying evidence, misleading grand juries, and other misconduct which most of the time goes unpunished."

One of the best analyses of prosecutorial misconduct comes from a series of ten articles in the Pittsburgh Post-Gazette in November and December of 1998. The newspaper reported:

"Hundreds of times during the past 10 years, federal agents and prosecutors have pursued justice by breaking the law. They lied, hid evidence, distorted facts, engaged in cover-ups, paid for perjury, and set up innocent people in a relentless effort to win indictments, guilty pleas, and convictions. Rarely were these federal officials punished for their misconduct...

"Perjury has become the coin of the realm in federal law enforcement. People's homes are invaded because of lies. People are arrested because of lies. People go to prison because of lies. People stay in prison because of lies, and bad guys go free because of lies."

Let's look at some high profile cases where prosecutors went astray in order to obtain desired convictions.

In the Exxon-Valdez case, the attorney general of the United States acknowledged that the felony charges against Exxon made, "a unique case which requires some innovative legal approaches which are never without risk." Innovative legal approaches can be assumed to mean violations of the constitution. This was a five count indictment.

1) One count charged Exxon with violating the Clean Water Act without a permit.
2) One count charged Exxon with violating the Refuse Act without a permit.

3) One count charged Exxon with violating hunting and killing migratory birds without a permit.
4) One count charged Exxon with violating the Posts and Waterways Act by "willfully and knowingly" employing people incapable of performing the duties assigned them.
5) One account charged Exxon with violating the Dangerous Cargo Act by "willfully and knowingly" employing people incapable of performing the duties assigned them.

Those charges were as phony as they could possibly be. On counts one and two, the incident was an accident so how could they have been expected to apply for a permit to violate the clean water act or dump refuge. On count #3, no one has suggested Exxon was planning to hunt and kill migratory birds so why should they have applied for a permit. Finally, on the final two counts, can anyone imagine Exxon intentionally hiring people who were not capable of performing their duties. No one had hired the captain with the expectation that he would be drunk while directing his ship.

Those charges meant that Exxon had intentionally committed these violations. They were all based on laws that had been adopted for purposes other than for which used.

In a front-page story on March 1, 1990. the New York Times said that "the government faces a risky criminal trial based on untested legal principles."

Exxon would almost surely have been exonerated in a proper trial but with the mighty media attack mounted by the environmentalists, Exxon plead guilty to avoid the publicity and bad press of a trial, and surrendered the opportunity to protect the constitution.

Charles H. Keating, Jr, a leading figure in the so-called Savings and Loan scandal, was convicted of a crime that was not on the books until he was charged with it. The prosecutors had taken a crime that was on the statute books as a civil offense and converted it into a felony, and Judge Lance Ito, later to be famous in the O.J. Simpson case, allowed it. Keating spent 4 ½ years in prison before a federal judge declared his conviction to be a violation of the constitutional prohibition of ex post facto law.

Clark Clifford was considered to be one of the most intelligent men in Washington, D.C for the past half century. He advised Presidents John F. Kennedy and Lyndon Johnson, served as the principal attorneys for numerous cases, had a major role in bringing about recognition of the nation of Israel and was one of the most honored men in Washington.

In 1992, an ambitious district attorney set his sights on the 80 year old Clifford and his younger partner Robert Altman, and indicted them for bank fraud relating to alleged bribes. The district attorney admitted he had no evidence on any victim – just a theory. After an investigation that cost taxpayers $10 million dollars, the indictments merely theorized that several legal and unremarkable individual transactions in which Clifford and Altman had engaged must have involved conspiracy and fraud. The judge found that there was nothing to the bribery theory. Clifford suffered a massive heart attack before the trial and the jury ruled that there was no evidence against Altman. Charges were dropped against Clifford because of lack of evidence.

It is not the large notorious cases which build impressive conviction percentages. That has to be done by achieving many, many convictions on which defense attorneys charge suborned perjury and other similar conduct.

Part II

True Professionals Recommend Effective Improvements

Five chapters explore the major improvements recommended by dedicated, highly professional lawyers as minimum steps to rebuilding an effective, honorable and worthy profession.

Chapter 17

Top Priority! Admit the Evidence

The most serious cancer in the entire judicial court system may be the exclusionary rule that was adopted by the Supreme Court in 1961. We join with important legal authorities in recommending (could we instead demand?) that it be eliminated as the first step in a logical legal reform. Our court system will function better if all factual evidence is admitted except for a few carefully defined situations.

In briefest form, the rule states that evidence obtained in violation of the Fourth Amendment should be excluded from a criminal trial. Nowhere in the constitution is there a hint that such evidence should be refused admittance. Instead, the U.S. Supreme Court first set the beginnings of the exclusionary rule for federal offices in 1914 but it was in 1961, under the leadership of Chief Justice Earl Warren, that the rule was extended so that it covered the police of every city and state. The court did not, however, define what types of actions might constitute violations of the amendment.

To fully understand how destructive the exclusionary rule has been, let us cite lists of detailed and particularized rules provided by Justice Burton S. Katz, that have evolved out of the 1961 decision. The list includes:

"rules for arrests, detentions, stop-and-frisk, searches of personal residences, searches of outbuildings, searches of third party premises, searches of third party personal effects, searches of trash cans while on the property of a suspect, searches of trash cans sitting on a sidewalk, searches of a trash can dumped into a truck but not yet mixed with other trash, searches after the trash has been dumped into a truck but that has been mixed with other trash, searches of parked automobiles, searches of automobiles that have been stopped, searches during flyovers, searches of open fields, searches of contraband in plain view, searches conducted pursuant to a warrant, searches conducted with consent of an accused, searches while in hot pursuit, searches conducted as a result of authorized wiretapping, searches conducted as a result of eavesdropping, body searches, multinational searches, searches that demand prompt attention, and searches conducted with the intent of preventing further bloodshed. If the police want to search a closed container, there are differing rules for closed lunch boxes, purses, footlockers, luggage cases, cardboard cartons, and paper bags."

All of these rules have been established through decisions by Supreme Courts (both federal and state) and appellate courts. Yet, they have not been written down and carefully worded except as they apply to a specific case. If the judges try to apply them to a different case with slightly different circumstances, the rules are subject to change and so they are constantly changing.

To further compound the confusion, the rules are different if they apply to a suspect as compared to a "probable cause" suspect (Yes, the courts have been able to discern a difference so differing rules apply.) Likewise, the rules change according to the state of mind of the police officer. And the rules are different from state to state.

The result has been that the rule has led to an infinite number of interpretations and no one can know whether a given action is permissible. The perceived violation may be so slight that it exists only in the mind of a defense attorney. As one example, an officer patrolling the streets of New York City was notified of a 911 call warning that a man was carrying a gun in violation of city law. An officer located the man, patted him down, found the gun and developed evidence of more substantial criminal activities. When the man was convicted, an appellate court threw out all charges against the man because the 911 call had been anonymous and the officer did not know who had supplied the information.

The exclusionary rule came about for the flimsiest of reasons and was based on a flaw in Supreme Court procedure. Like a growing cancer, the rule has been steadily expanded even though relying on unsound roots.

Former Supreme Court Justice Byron White predicted that the courts would not be satisfied until all evidence obtained from an individual suspected of a crime, whether voluntarily or not, had been barred from admission to a court of justice.

Fortunately, eliminating the rule would not require amending the constitution because these are man-made problems and it would simply take an act by Congress and signature by the president. Or the changes could come about by a willingness of the courts to correct the problem.

Two aspects of the problem exist. First, the exclusionary rule must be eradicated. There is simply no way that an intelligent nation, intending to restore a fair and effective justice system, can do so without that action. Secondly, methods must be provided whereby the accused will be protected against overzealous police action.

The arguments here will be couched in terms expressed by three justices in highly responsible positions. That will maintain the legal terminology.

"...The hallmarks of the exclusionary rule are irrationalities, arbitrariness, and a lack of proportion. When it is applied, a criminal goes free – no matter how serious the crime or minor the police intrusion. The bald fact is that it is more lottery than law."

So wrote New York Supreme Court Justice Harold Rothwax, Jr.

Former Supreme Court Justice Hugo Black earlier expressed his opinion,

"The Fourth Amendment prohibits unreasonable search and seizures. The amendment does not say anything about consequences. It certainly nowhere provides for the exclusion of evidence as the remedy for violation."

Justice John L. Kane, Jr. of the U.S. District court of Colorado, concurs:

"The first and most glaring rule which should be eliminated is the exclusion of illegally obtained evidence. Clearly, the rule is the enemy of truth and the truth-seeking process."

A case in Manchester, New Hampshire, illustrated the unjustness of the rule. 14 year old Pamela Mason earned money by baby-sitting after school and evenings. On January 13, 1964, she received a telephone call from a man who had seen her notice on the bulletin board at the local laundromat. That bulletin board was the source of most of her jobs and the caller wanted to hire her for the evening.

When Pamela arrived home from school, her mother was leaving for her job as a waitress. She told her daughter that the man had promised to call back and at 4:30, the telephone rang. Pamela's younger brother answered the call and although he did not overhear the conversation, he was able to confirm that the caller was a man. Pamela left the house soon after 6:00 PM and her family would never see her alive again.

Eight days later, Pamela's frozen body was discovered in a snowdrift beside an interstate highway a few miles from her home. Her throat had been slashed and she had been shot in the head. Medical evidence showed that she had died somewhere between 8:00 and 10:00 PM on the night that she disappeared.

In the manhunt that followed, two witnesses told police that at 9:30 on the night of the murder, they had paused to offer assistance to a man in a 1951 Pontiac that was stopped on the highway near where Pamela's body was found.

Edward Coolidge owned a 1951 Pontiac that matched the description of the vehicle seen near the location of the body. A neighbor reported that the man had been absent from home between 5:00 and 11:00 PM on the night of the murder.

When police went to Coolidge's house to question him 15 days after the murder, he claimed that he had been shopping in a nearby town on the night in question. He also admitted that he was a frequent customer of the laundromat, and that he had been there on the night of the murder. He readily showed them three guns.

Later two different officers, not aware of the first visit, went to the home and asked if there were any guns in the house. Mrs. Coolidge showed them four guns and allowed them to take the weapons plus various articles of clothing for testing. One of the guns proved to be the murder weapon.

As the evidence accumulated, the police chief swore under oath that there was probable cause justifying a search of the automobile that had been parked in the driveway and requested a search warrant. The state attorney general who had taken charge of the investigation, signed the search warrant while acting as justice of the peace as he was authorized to do under New Hampshire law. Vacuum sweepings from the car as well as from the clothing proved that Pamela's body had been in the trunk. Edward Coolidge was subsequently arrested.

In the trial that followed, four different persons testified that the suspect had asked them to fabricate a false alibi for the night of the murder. Coolidge was convicted and sentenced to life in prison. The police had taken every precaution to assure that a search warrant had been obtained.

How could the Supreme Court possibly find reason to throw out the life sentence? It found a way as it made the decision that the search warrant had not been issued by a "neutral and detached magistrate" but by a law enforcement officer even though he was acting as a justice of the peace in accordance with prevailing law. "Searches outside the judicial process, without prior approval by judge or magistrate, are per se unreasonable under the Fourth Amendment subject only to a few specifically established and well-defined exceptions." Even though the police could properly have made a search of the car without a warrant in the driveway when they arrested Coolidge, they could not have done so at their leisure after the car was removed to their holding facilities. Talk about splitting hairs! To explain this fine point of interpretation, the court provided a

43 page explanation, and it denied the right to submit evidence from the automobile in further trial.

The killer went free. The Supreme Court had made a joke out of interpretation of the Constitution and Edward Coolidge won the lottery on a minor technical point. The records are full of cases where convictions have been set aside on seemingly harmless technicalities.

The widespread application of the exclusionary rule came into being as a decision on an appeal of the conviction of Dolly Mapp whose name became pivotal in the history of the criminal court system. She lived on the upper floor of a two story brick house in Cleveland, Ohio and rented out rooms to boarders.

Three police officers came to her place searching for a man in connection with a recent bombing. After consulting her attorney on the phone, Mrs Mapp told the officers she wouldn't admit them without a search warrant. Three hours later, the officers came back and forced their way into her home. She demanded to see a warrant and one officer showed her a piece of paper. Without looking at it, she shoved it down the front of her blouse. A struggle followed in which the officers attempted to retrieve the paper. Finally, the officers handcuffed Mrs. Mapp and went on with their search. The wanted man was not found and the paper turned out not to be a search warrant.

In the search, however, the officers discovered four books which they considered to be pornographic material. Dolly Mapp was convicted on possession of obscene materials and after approval at the Appeals Court, the case went to the U.S. Supreme Court to test the law on pornography.

The appeal claimed several issues but improper search and seizure was not even on the list of issues that were part of the appeal.

Normal Supreme Court procedure is for a conference to be held during which the contending attorneys are allotted a specific time in which to make their arguments and explain their cases. Neither of the parties to the appeal even brought up the matter of search and seizure. Later, with attorneys absent, the nine justices discussed the case as is normal practice until five members had agreed that the conviction would be reversed on the grounds of the first and the fourteenth amendments (free speech and due process). In accordance with normal practice, one member of the court, this time Justice Tom Clark, was assigned to write the majority opinion. That opinion would later be submitted for signature to the five members who had agreed to overturn the case.

This time, four members of the court, one short of the needed majority, apparently met in private session to decide that the opinion should be written not based on the first and fourteenth amendments as the court had agreed, but on a version of their own choosing, namely to base the opinion on the fourth amendment, illegal search and seizure.

When that opinion reached the desk of Justice Potter Stuart, he was shocked that the reversal on the case was based not on the First and Fourteenth Amendments as the justices had agreed, but on the Fourth Amendment, the one that forbad illegal search and seizure and which had not even been under consideration by the court. Stewart communicated his concern that an important doctrine was being overturned that hadn't even been discussed. He could apparently have withheld his signature until the opinion was based on the issues as agreed but he didn't.

Still, a majority of the justices agreed that the decision of the lower court should be overturned and the court schedules did not permit sending the matter back for rewriting. The reversal stood and the written opinion gave us the unreasonable, trouble causing rule that no evidence can be admitted if found by illegal search and seizure. In no previous ruling ever made by the Supreme Court had that meant that the evidence could not be submitted at trial.

New York Judge Frank Weissberg has summarized,

"The law on search and seizure is so unpredictable that if my only concern was being affirmed by the appellate court, without regard to the merits of the case, I don't think I could be sure of that result more than 60 per cent of the time."

Before we offer arguments by some authorities on law, let us remind that all too often, high level justices on the Supreme Court and Appeals courts are more often politicians with an agenda than true legal scholars. It is apparent that the four justices had a political agenda.

For additional knowledgeable comment, we continue with Justice Rothwax:

"...If you're looking for the major culprit in the malaise-ridden justice system, ...look at the convoluted way the Courts have interpreted the Fourth Amendment

"It is impossible for the Court to establish rules that would govern all future cases because when one rule is established, the next case is different.

"Police officers do not have the time, inclination or training to read and understand the nuances of appellate decisions that define standards of conduct...The legal doctrines (that) the exclusionary rule enforces are so complicated and tangled that the police and the judges themselves cannot determine in advance what a majority of the Supreme Court will find."

Another thorough discussion was provided by John Kane.

"The presupposition is that if evidence is excluded and the prosecution's case is thereby either extinguished or severely hampered even to the extent that guilty people might go free, law enforcement officials will not engage in such conduct."

"To exclude relevant facts in the search for truth is a slur of gigantic proportions on every foundation of a democratic society."

"Let us look for a moment at the great differences between our rules of procedure and reality...Rule 1 of the Federal Rules of Civil Procedure says that the Rules shall be construed to secure the just, speedy and inexpensive determination of every action...The rules and procedures that we use frequently require or at least encourage unethical behavior on our part... In repeated instances, we are seen as enemies of the truth rather than as champions of it...Change must be instituted or the system will collapse of its own irrelevance.

"Many of the complaints about lawyer competence are rooted in the impossibility of anyone being able to cope with the inadequacies of the system...Truth is not being realized or recognized as a product of the legal system. People are committing crimes and they are not being held accountable. Criminals are set free and police officers are punished,.

"Rule 102 of the Federal Rules of Evidence says: These rules shall be construed to secure fairness in administration, elimination of unjustifiable growth and development of the law of evidence to the end that the truth may be ascertained and proceedings justly determined...Despite the piety with which these aspirational statements are frequently chanted, an examination of the text and practice of the law establishes quite clearly that indeed the search for truth is not the purpose at all. The development of the law of evidence has been one (toward) a point of view of favoring the exclusion of evidence (as opposed to) one favoring it's inclusion...

"The basic principle...is that all relevant evidence is admissible except that which is specifically excluded by rule or statute. The test for relevance is quite simple: Relevant evidence means evidence having any tendency to make the existence of the fact that is of consequence to the principle is that jurors have the right to consider all facts which may assist them in determining the truth.

"The justification of the role excluding relevant evidence in criminal cases because it deters illegal police conduct is just plain silly. First and foremost, is that police officers are not evaluated on their performance of duty on the basis of what some magistrate may rule as a matter of hindsight. If the truth be known, the officer receives praise for his quick action from his peers and the magistrate is scorned by them for absurdly countenancing criminal conduct. Decisions about the job stability and future success of police officers are made by command personnel, not by judges, prosecutors or legislatures.

"Second, trial judges have never enforced the exclusionary rule with consistency or collective enthusiasm. Third, appellate judges have never been able to articulate a coherent rule to which law enforcement officers in the crucible of action can adhere or trial judges in the press of trial can enforce. Fourth, legislative reference personnel, legislators, and academics have never evaluated the consequences of this rule in terms of human costs or efficacy.

"Truth is sacrificed and the higher value is ignored. The constitution does not require the exclusionary rule."

We come again to the concept that the most crucial purposes of our judicial system should be to determine truth. Is the accused guilty or innocent? Truth is the existence or non-existence of a fact. The aim should not be to create a set of rules for some awe-inspiring game wherein the principal purpose of participation is to determine which person can abide by those rules and which is to operate outside the boundaries. Can we manufacture a reason, be it ever so small, that the rules have been transgressed? Can we find another excuse that I should release a potential prisoner because some rule was violated under the guise of a violation of his rights?

Continuing with Kane:

"Rules of evidence which exclude should only be formulated, justified, or invoked on the basis of its trustworthiness. In the event a policy is to be invoked because there is a value considered greater then the truth that is desired, which is to say a value intended to predominate over the truth, the policy should be clearly enunciated and the jury should be clearly instructed that their search of the truth is subordinated to that end."

Lester Langford, Chief of Police of Cherry Hills Village, a suburb of Denver, Colorado, expressed his dismay with,

"I just look at our government, how big and huge it has become, and what was intended by our founding fathers. It is so far afield from what our founding fathers intended that if they should come back and visit this and see the attorneys arguing over the technicalities and the loopholes of this court system, they would be totally revolted. We have suspects caught on tape committing crimes and yet we go to trial to argue about whether or not they are guilty...Our founding fathers would absolutely roll over in their graves."

Professor William Pizzi of the school of law at the University of Colorado likened the modern trial to a game of football frequently interrupted by the fluttering of little yellow flags, often followed by conclaves of officials trying to reach agreement on the appropriate ruling.

"As I watch important criminal cases unfold on television, I see trials that are covered just like sporting events, complete with color commentators and lots of Monday morning quarterbacking, while it may be entertaining and even captivating at times, I question whether what I am seeing is a strong trial system.

"A country...has only one court system. But a country cannot be so inclusive when it comes to trial systems because a trial system does not exist to entertain the public or showcase the skills of the legal players. A trial system must strive to achieve much more difficult objectives. No trial system is a strong one if it cannot be trusted to acquit the innocent and convict the guilty with a high degree of reliability."

THE EXCLUSIONARY RULE MUST BE ELIMINATED. That must be the highest priority alteration to be made in the legal system. Without doing so, there can be no realistic reform of the criminal court system.

It follows though that any suggestion to admit evidence obtained through illegal search and seizure must be accompanied by strong restraints to protect the individual against unwarranted transgressions by the police in violation of the fourth amendment

Judge Rothwax recommends a common sense approach to the serious matter of search and seizure. The biggest single fault of the exclusionary rule is that it is mandatory. Rothwax would ask that when a question of admissible evidence is raised by the defense, the presiding judge should consider several issues regarding the specific evidence and should then make a decision. These concerns would be the impact of the following issues: probable cause, existence or non-existence of a search warrant, a need for quick action, the seriousness of the crime, the amount of evidence involved, the nature of the police search and the possible dangerous nature of the accused.

To the issues listed by Judge Rothwax, I would suggest that it should be considered whether a good faith effort was made to obtain a proper search warrant. Too many search warrants have been disapproved on technicalities.

Every officer when charged with violating the civil rights of an accused should understand that he or she is going to be judged on whether the actions were reasonable. It would not necessarily mean that he went through every issue or even most of them before he made the decision to proceed on the development of evidence.

If the police officer is prepared to defend at least the most relevant questions like; Is there probable cause? Were there feasible reasons that made obtaining a search warrant unfeasible? What was the seriousness of the crime under investigation? On consideration of those three questions, the officer may well be judged not to have violated the defendant's civil rights.

If the four police officers who scaled the wall at O.J. Simpson's Rockingham estate be considered to have reasonably considered Rothwax's areas pf concern, would they, logically have been considered to have been making an acceptable entry? If Simpson had been convicted, an appeal would undoubtedly have been made on the claim of exclusionable evidence. We can be certain that the court would then have overturned the verdict on some minor violation of the rules and a new trial would have been ordered.

Judge Rothwax's proposal would have worked very well indeed if the improper Supreme Court ruling in the MAPP case had never occurred and if we hadn't gone through forty years of experience working with the exclusionary rule and it's unfortunate results. Those who are so paranoid about overzealousness of the police officers would never stand for such a reasonable set of restraints.

Judge Kane would take a more formalized approach to protect an accused against illegal search and seizure.

"Given the proven ability of the federal government to license airplane pilots, or regulate interstate truck drivers or certify able-bodied seamen, there is no reason why a simple certification process for law enforcement officers could not be established. The constitution does not require the exclusionary rule. A government which can suspend, restrict, or cancel the certification of a pilot who has performed a dangerous or unauthorized maneuver with an aircraft is fully capable of imposing similar sanctions on errant police officers who violate the constitutional rights of individuals whether intentionally, habitually or serendipitously. The fear that such a role cannot be entrusted to the federal government because it would intrude unnecessarily into state action is groundless. State and local governments, including law enforcement agencies, employ pilots who must be licensed. The federal government issues the license to the pilot. It does not tell the state or local government which pilot must be hired.

"It is obvious that untrained and undisciplined police officers cause more injuries to the public than do unlicensed pilots if for no other reason than that there are more of them."

Like Justice Rothwax's plan, Justice Kane's offering would be an effective proposal but my prediction would be that vocal critics who continually claim victimization would politicize every trial. They would demand that the police be charged with violations on too many actions.

Chief Lester Langford of Cherry Hills, Colorado described a different method that would maintain state or municipal police under proper restrictions.

"In Colorado, the licensing process is conducted by the Post Board, (police officer selection and training). Every prospective police officer goes through hundreds of hours of classroom training as a beginning step. Then the police officer goes through a field officer's training program. Finally, only after the police officer is hired as a full time police officer can the candidate be state certified. That state certificate is subject to revocation if the person does certain things. Possibly, the area to control violations of the fourth amendment would be to strengthen that to where sustained violations against an officer are noted and forwarded to the POST board and after a certain number of points or after a certain number of violations, the officer's certificate would be revoked.

The various methods of protection would each have advantages and disadvantages. The advantage of local punishment would be that it would leave intact the local control over the police force. This would entail the continued threat of federal intervention in cases of civil rights violations and that threat could be the powerful enforcement principle that is needed.

The disadvantage to this system is that with 50 states, we would end up with 50 state laws and with 50 different levels of enforcement. But that is true of all state criminal actions. Different laws provide different legal trails.

The question that has not yet been addressed is the matter whether knocking out the exclusionary rule is possible. Since it was originated and invoked by the Supreme court, is the foundation so firm that we can not even chisel at it? Certain high level judges only a step away from the Supreme Court have certainly believed that it can be done.

More importantly, if it gains adequate support among the voting public, the change can come about slowly but firmly. It is too much in conflict with democratic principles for it to stand in opposition to a firm will of the people.

In addition to elimination of the rule excluding evidence obtained by illegal search and seizure, Judge Kane also proposes as follows: Reconsideration of the following types of exclusion:

1. Exclusion of evidence showing the amount or existence of insurance coverage.
2. Exclusion of evidence of previous criminal convictions.

3. Exclusion of evidence showing previous sexual conduct
4. Exclusion of evidence of other business transactions.
5. The attorney's work-product.
6. Communication by employees to in-house counsel
7. Details of settlement with other parties.
8. Exclusion of evidence of repair or change of procedure after injuries or accidents occur.
9. Payment of medical or other expenses.
10. Exclusion of Census Information
11. The Attorney-Client Privilege
12. The Doctor-Client Privilege
13. The Priest-Confessor Privilege
14. The Husband-Wife Privilege.

"The foregoing exclusions tend to foster an exclusive effect on the truth seeking process. They enforce the belief that truth is not the desired end of the legal process and that jurors are lacking in the ability to deal with the truth.

"We prohibit introduction of an accused's record of felony convictions for the stated reason that a jury would be prejudiced into believing it is more probable than not that a person who committed crimes will commit more crimes. Imagine that...Who could possibly believe that a person who has committed crimes in the past is more likely to commit crimes in the future? An unbelievable assumption!

"Truth is meant to mean the existence or non-existence of a fact...The establishment of facts must be the precursor of decision. To do otherwise is to pervert the process and to insure that the conclusion reached is wrong because it is based on insufficient data...The (current) process leads to distinctions which are lacking in common sense and thus lacking become the subject of public scorn and ridicule."

I could reasonably see abolishing all of the above exclusionary relationships listed above by Justice Kane except the priest-confessor and possibly the attorney-client privilege.

As Professor Craig Bailey of the Indiana University School of Law has pointed out, requiring police officers to use their common sense, and judging them by that standard, seems more likely to produce sensible results than does a set of unknowable rules and vague exceptions that neither the police nor the courts can understand.

The intent of the proposed change in judicial practice is to admit all of the evidence no matter how obtained unless it is thrown out for the reason of being false evidence. Examples of false evidence would be a written document that is forged, physical evidence that has been implanted, or conversations which can be proven never to have occurred.

Under the proposed rules, all evidence would have been accepted. The goal is truth, not fancy games.

━ ∙ ━ ∙ ━ ∙ ━ ∙ ━ ∙ ━ ∙ ━ ∙ ━ ∙ ━ ∙ ━ ∙ ━ ∙ ━

Since I wrote an earlier version proposing these same changes, I could, of course, have written this chapter in my own words. It will be difficult enough to persuade the legal community to accept the concepts presented here when written by authoritative lawyers. It wouldn't have stood a chance of being accepted if the parallel but near identical concepts had been offered as being originated by me.

As I stated previously, Judge Rothwax's proposal would have been a desirable alternative to the Exclusionary Rule if that rule had not been in effect for 40 years. Citizens have developed too much of a habit of protesting every judgmental approach.

At the time of my earlier writing, I probably would have chosen a method very similar to that proposed by Chief Langford to leave the oversight in the hands of the local jurisdictions.

If today, however, I were to state a preference, it would be for the method described by Judge Kane to place the federal government squarely as a protection against the feared overzealousness.

Chapter 18

Admit the Confessions

Stare decisis is the principle in law whereby the precedent of previous decisions in similar cases by the same court or by courts superior to it in the same judicial system which had jurisdiction, should be followed if the precedent is currently applicable. By following that principle, brick by brick, our court system has built a massive foundation of legal doctrine with roots as far back as the Common Law of England. These principles can theoretically be negated by changes in the constitution or by statutes legislated into law.

Nowhere does the Fifth Amendment require that an accused cannot be questioned without an attorney. Instead, it says that he shall not be "compelled in a criminal case to be a witness against himself". Questioning is not compulsion. The Sixth Amendment states that "In all criminal prosecutions, the accused shall enjoy the right to a speedy and public trial...and to have the Assistance of Counsel for his Defense." It does not say that he has the right to counsel every time that he is questioned. He is not being prosecuted until charges are filed. It is one of the fictions issued by the court that he is being prosecuted as soon as he is questioned.

Stare decisis is not of itself a bad practice but when a faulty decision is rendered and then ensuing courts build on that flawed decision in case after case over many decades, some future result may become one of the root causes of some evil, the growth of crime as the most formidable example. For 175 years of our nation's history, the decisions in regard to confessions had been treated reasonably well by the courts but with an illogical set of precedents beginning to develop in the pathway of stare decisis.

Attorneys insist on examining the meaning of different words and then offering very fluid definitions of what the word means on the legal landscape.

The word that is at the heart of endless problems in complying with the constitution is the word "compel". Every dictionary definition refers to the use of force as being a basic meaning of the word. How much pressure constitutes force? What kinds of pressures constitute force? The Supreme Court has gone the route of declaring that any words or action that persuade can be classified as force.

Does verbal trickery constitute force? Does nudging a person's conscience constitute force? Does the presence of fear, even though not intentionally caused by a police officer, constitute force? Does awe of being in the presence of a police officer constitute fear? Would relating a story with a moral constitute force? Would blinking an eye constitute force? No such decision has yet come out of the higher courts but it would be totally in line with past decisions.

An example of where the word "compel" was taken to have an overbroad definition was the much analyzed "Christian burial" case. On Christmas Eve, 1968, 10 year old Pamela Powers disappeared from a YMCA event in Des Moines, Iowa. A man was seen carrying a wrapped bundle to his car with a pair of legs extended from the bundle. Later that car was found abandoned in Davenport, about 160 miles away. In the car, police found ample conclusive evidence including Pamela's clothing.

Robert Williams telephoned a Des Moines lawyer and said that he knew that the police were looking for him. After Williams turned himself in to police, a judge ordered that he be transported back to Des Moines.

Two officers, one of them Captain Leaming, went after Williams and were in the process taking him back to Des Moines. The attorney for Williams told the officers, "Don't talk to him. Don't question him. He's represented by counsel now. He's been arraigned; and so you mustn't talk to him."

On the way back to Des Moines, it began to snow. The snow began to fall harder and harder until it was a total blizzard.

Captain Leaming knew that Robert Williams was an escaped mental patient of strong religious tendencies.

With the snow falling hard, the captain commented, "Reverend Williams, you know that I am not supposed to question you and I am not going to question you. But I have something that I wanted to mention. It's a concern of mine. Just think about what I am saying, but don't respond, please"

"It's snowing like crazy and pretty soon the ground will be covered with snow. It's Christmas time. I'm sure this family would like to have a good Christian burial for their child. I guess, if you don't know where the child is, there's no point of mentioning it. But if you do, it's probably your last chance to give this family a Christian burial for their daughter. I just want you to think about that."

Some hours later, as they neared the end of their trip, Williams said, "Okay, let me take you to the body." And he guided them to the place where he had buried Pamela in a ditch. Scientific evidence showed that Pamela had been sexually assaulted and smothered.

Williams was convicted and when the case was taken to the federal court, the conviction was overturned because the captain had violated William's rights. It could hardly be said that Captain Leaming compelled the accused to take him to the body. He did mentally manipulate Williams' thought pattern and the verdict was overturned because of it.

In another case two officers walked up to a man standing behind a car on a city street. Without any threatening words from the officers, the man suddenly blurted out that there was a body in the trunk of the car. They then obtained a search warrant and went into the trunk where they found the dismantled parts of a female body. After the man was convicted of murder, the higher courts overthrew the conviction because the man had been "intimidated" by the presence of police and lost his composure.

As more and more cases go through the court, more and more meanings become involved in never ending permutations, forever leading to more numerous reversals.

Although in a subsequent chapter, I will severely condemn the principal teachings of Jeremy Bentham, one of his arguments from 175 years ago is now presented as an argument against an accused person being given an equal opportunity to escape punishment:

> "Pursuing criminal justice is not a fox hunt. We should place every advantage in favor of carrying out criminal justice short of seriously violating the person's constitutional rights. We, the citizenry, should want the fox to be caught."

Called the fairness doctrine or the fox-hunter's argument, this concept was criticized by Bentham when he wrote:

> "The fox is to have a fair chance for his life: He must have what is called in law: …leave to run a certain length of way, for the express purpose of giving him a chance for escape. While under pursuit, he must not be shot…It would be unfair as convicting him of burglary on a hen roost, in five minutes' time, in a court of conscience."

Bentham observed that giving an accused man this kind of opportunity to avoid a confession and so escape conviction in a trial would make sense only if the trial process was being conducted under some kind of sporting code.

As illogical as that concept might seem, case followed case in which the idea of fairness grew. In developing the pattern for a game, rules must be established which cause both sides in the contest to have a fair chance to win. But efforts to control and eliminate crime are not a game. What an undermining concept that the contest between police officer and an accused should be fair! If a criminal shot and killed another person, did he or she provide a fair chance to the victim? Or if he robbed a victim at gunpoint, did he make sure that he followed rules of fair play for armed robbery? Why then should fairness be a factor in the apprehension of a perpetrator?

The proponents of a fair chance have been concerned that the accused person did not have equal knowledge of the law compared to the police questioner, or he might be unaware that he had the right to an attorney, or he might not understand that he could not be forced to testify against himself.

Nowhere in the Bill of Rights was there a hint that fair play and equality should be factors in the apprehension of criminals. Only by a process of evolutionary cases on the basis of stare decisis could such a concept develop. Instead the constitution says that an accused cannot be compelled to testify against himself. Fair play and compulsion are far different and therein lies one of the corruptions brought about by the court review system.

Yet there obviously must be limits to how far the police can go to avoid having an act judged as compulsion. The fairness concept would indeed be applicable if the police were wanting to question an eight year old boy on a charge of murder. He should unquestionably be allowed to have his parents present. Indeed the very matter of such a juvenile being in a room alone with a police officer could be so intimidating it would meet any reasonable definition of compulsion.

There was a real case where a 14 year old culprit and his two younger friends, broke into the apartment of an elderly man, beat him to the extent that he later died, and robbed him of $13. The three friends were recognized from descriptions of the culprit and apprehended. The officer invited the oldest of the three brothers into the car. He almost immediately confessed to assault and robbery, repeated it the following day and almost a week later signed the confession. Although the Miranda ruling was still four years in the future, the police officer had, nevertheless advised him that he had a right to counsel, the right to remain silent and the right to have his family present.

The Supreme Court reviewed the case, taking particular note of the convicted man's age, and overthrew the conviction in Gallegos v. Colorado with emphasis on failure of the police officers to grant parents immediate access to him. "We deal with a person who is not equal to the police in knowledge and understanding." Yet they ignored the fact that he had signed the confession several days after the event and several days after he had talked to his parents.

This was the first known instance where the Supreme Court based the overthrow of a conviction on the defendant not being equal to police. But the principle was thus planted and made available to be expanded for future cases.

Later, there came the case where it was not a single convicted person but two 21 year old youths. This time the principle of imbalance is not based on a minor against the cops but the fact that the questioning combined a bit of trickery on the part of police in that they kept the two youths separated. They left one alone for an hour and when they returned, a secretary accompanied the officers writing on her note pad. As she proceeds, she asks the young man in front of her how he spells his last name. The young man assumes that his accomplice has confessed and so, proceeds to tell the police the entire story. Ah, says the appeals court. Here is that matter of imbalance that the court had used as a basis in those previous cases. The confession was thrown out and that overturned the conviction. The question by the secretary had been deemed to go somewhat beyond fairness.

Cases followed in which the court more and more began to claim that a voluntary confession must be obtained fairly as if it were a sporting contest rather than a search for the truth. It was not a matter of a few crucial cases but rather a gradual climb over multiple cases toward restricting police conduct to achieve fairness.

The case of Escobedo v. Illinois arrived in which the accused was believed to have shot his brother-in-law and was questioned at length before his attorney secured his release. More than a week later, police were informed by another suspect that Escobedo had been the killer. Soon in further questioning when the men were face to face, Escobedo exclaimed, "I didn't shoot Manuel. You did it." Those words were a confession that he had direct knowledge of the killing. He had pushed past the earlier advice of his attorney who had told him what not to do in the face of further police interrogation.

Rules for police conduct were being developed and put into effect over the police enforcement community but, even if an officer followed the existing rules, the courts were still rendering verdicts to overthrow confessions.

In a similar vein, the understandings vary as to when the requirement begins that a possible defendant becomes entitled to counsel. Some like Supreme Court Justice Harlon Stone contends that it starts at the beginning of an adversarial procedure which means at the beginning of a trial, others contending that it should begin when the accused is arraigned, or when charges are filed against him. Still others feel that it should start when interrogation is initiated with the person being in custody.

With each case that reached the Supreme Court, a decision was reached that extended the idea a little closer to a required equality in behalf of the questioned. Then came the infamous, wrong-headed Miranda case, which placed long term burdens on interrogators.

An activist Supreme Court decided to implant the equality as a permanent rule of law and it issued what would, in the future, be known as the Miranda Rule. That dictate of law imposed not only equality but even a possible imbalance in favor of the accused. The representative for the accused must be a lawyer but the questioner may be no more than a clerk for the police.

Ernesto Miranda had been arrested for rape of a teenage girl but she could not identify him from a police lineup. Following the lineup, Miranda asked a policeman, "How did I do?" "You flunked," came the reply.

Miranda was questioned for two hours and confessed, not only to the crime under investigation but to another rape as well. Police brought the teenage girl into the interrogation room and Miranda, believing that she had identified him, said, "That's the girl."

Three years later, the Supreme Court, being concerned that the police had manipulated Miranda into a confession, overturned his conviction. There had been no claim of compulsion but the court believed that the balance of fairness had been tipped. Did they really need to be fair?

The Supreme Court chose that case to issue a rigid standard to address the ever-returning issue of fairness.

The court declared that, prior to questioning, the police must warn a suspect in custody, that he has a right to remain silent, any statements the accused makes might be used against him, and that he has the right to the presence of counsel. If he does not have one, one will be appointed for him. If the police failed to give warning, any statement, however voluntary, would be used against him. Custodial interrogations were the concern. Once any question was asked, any response would be barred unless the warning was given and a waiver obtained.

The court wrote a discourse of fifty pages describing the meaning of the new rule before they took up the case then under consideration. The courts do not normally discuss issues and opinions extensively unless that analysis applies directly to the decision. This action by the Supreme Court went far beyond allowable limits. In comment, even liberal Supreme Court Justice Tom Clarke said, "No sane person would knowingly relinquish the right to be free of compulsion."

Rather than using a fixed rule that goes so far in trying to free every accused, could we agree that by limiting the meaning of compulsion to the following practices proposed by some judges, we would provide a suitably precise meaning of the word "compulsion" - prolonged detention – threats - physical force – relay questioning – financial inducement - denial of food - denial of sleep – intimidation. There should even be room for some of those to depend on a matter of degree.

If methods are used to bring forth a confession that do not shock the conscience of a reasonable person in regard to the listed inducements, then the confession should be judged to be "voluntary" and accepted into evidence.

But if any of those inducements are used to an extent or severity that the conscience of a reasonable person would be affronted, then the police officer who violated proper limits should be prosecuted for a felony. Even that, however, should not mean that the confessions should be disallowed as evidence. In the absence of any of those practices, however, compulsion should be assumed not to have occurred.

The thousands of variations which can be conceived make the law a never solved mystery. Another frustrating, much argued question is that the Supreme Courts has divided legal decisions into two categories, those that involve a violation of constitutional rights and those that are prophylactic rulings. The prophylactic rulings are intended to provide conditions which assure that there will be no violations of the Sixth Amendment. In other words, if the Miranda statement has been read to the person under restraint, they can be sure that the Sixth Amendment has not been violated. But if the Miranda warning has not been provided, that does not mean that the person's rights have automatically been violated. Even if the rights have been violated, however, the confession should still be admitted into evidence. The court still has to decide if there was a "conclusive presumption of compulsion." And if there was, the police officer should be punished. The confession should not be rejected.

Professor Joseph D. Grano, a foremost spokesman for the illegitimacy of the Miranda ruling has given us a predominant, highly technical book, *"Confessions, Truth and the Law"*, that analyzes the legal process leading up to the Miranda Decision and evaluates the unwanted results that it can provide. The professor's arguments totally support elimination of the Miranda Decision as improper and advocates that it should be removed from the legal guidelines.

Grano states,

"The court's description of Miranda as prophylactic, meaning...that the admission of a confession at trial may violate Miranda without violating the Fifth Amendment" and "...the court has never seen fit to explain its source of authority to impose the prophylactic characterization of Miranda without giving any thought to the legitimacy issue."

One of his strongest statements is,

"What makes Miranda illegitimate, is that the Court, according to its own admission, has exceeded the bounds of what the Constitution, interpreted by the Court, actually requires."

Has the justice system been better since adopting the Miranda rule? One evaluation of the share of violent crimes solved before and after the Miranda ruling was performed by law professor Paul Cassell and economist Richard Fowles at the University of Utah The results were published in the Stanford Law Review.

A definition of "crimes solved" was needed and certainly they couldn't rely on the percentage of court convictions. Instead, they based their study on cases where the police considered the case completed. Even though an accused might be found not guilty, if the police considered the facts sufficiently convincing that they could see no value in continuing to investigate the case, then it was considered to be solved. The FBI was the source of the information.

In the 1960s before the Miranda ruling, the percentage completions in cases of violent crimes varied between 60% and 64%. After 1968, the percentages of cases solved dropped to 43% to 46%. That means that hundreds of thousands of violent criminals are loose on the streets that wouldn't be there if there had been no Miranda rule. The attached graph shows the decline in completions of violent crime cases.

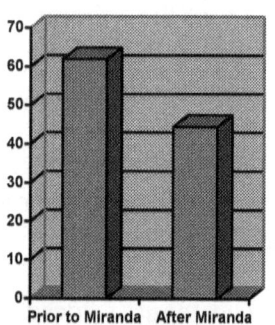

Effects of Miranda
Study by Cassell & Fowles

Percentage of Criminal Cases Solved

Before we leave the subject, the rules properly dictate that in the courtroom, when at trial, fairness is ordered by the constitution. A barrier to a reasonable definition of compulsion must exist in the investigative phase but equality must rule during the trial phase.

That's the way the non-lawyers see it. Today, the fox has an equal chance to escape. The odds may even be in his favor. That is not a logical approach to fighting crime!

It was earlier mentioned that one of the methods by which stare decisis could be overruled was that the Miranda ruling had been made inoperative by a statute passed by Congress and signed by the president. Congress soon passed and President Lyndon B. Johnson signed the Omnibus Crime Control and Safe Street Act of 1968.

Section 3501 of the federal criminal code was enacted which allowed prosecutors to introduce voluntary confessions into evidence even though the warning may not have been delivered. It allows federal judges to determine voluntariness by considering all of the circumstances, including the defendants knowledge of his rights and the presence or absence of Miranda warnings. The statute explicitly states that the defendant's lack of knowledge and absence of warnings need not be conclusive in determining voluntariness.

In effect, the Supreme Court simply ignored the statute and, since most police officers were, by then, trained to give the Miranda warning, treated the statute as though it is still in full effect. The result has been that in spite of the standing that a statute has traditionally held as a block to stare decisis, it is now assumed that a stare decisis rule can only be changed by a constitutional amendment. In other words, if he courts choose to run roughshod over a statute of law, any violations can be ignored.

Further, many legal authorities, such as former Chief Justice Warren Burger who formerly opposed the Miranda rule, said that the rule was a flawed rule to begin with, but since it has been in effect for 45 years and most officers have been trained to comply with it, we simply let it stand. If placed into effect, the Supreme Court is very likely to rule that the entire law is unconstitutional but it certainly is a move in the direction that the people seek.

It has become clear that the courts have revised the constitution without amendment when the majority of the members wish to pursue a political agenda but such change becomes unconstitutional when proper justice in pursuit of real truth would be served. Lawyers can uncover enough diversity in the meaning of words, to dispute any statement that is made.

Let's propose a logical and reasonable guideline. If an accused confesses a crime without being subjected to an extent of compulsion that would have offended a reasonable person in regard to the amount of prolonged detention, threats, physical force, relay questioning, financial inducement, denial of food, denial of sleep, or intimidation, then the confession should be admitted into evidence. Numerous judges and lawyers would accept that measure of admissibility.

Chapter 19

Use Reason in Judging Temporary Insanity

Possibly the greatest abuse of the American court system is the wildly irrational use of the plea of "Not guilty by reason of temporary insanity." This is a chapter that doesn't fit nicely into Part 2 because the partial remedies have apparently not been generated by even the best of attorneys but instead have been forced by the rumblings of politics. And to place it in Part 3 would mean that I had developed some creative ideas on how to correct the evil. The only original contribution that I could make is to recommend changing the designation of the pleading and finding from "Innocent by Reason of Insanity" to "Guilty with Allowance for Defect of Reason" or something similar. It should be something that carries the connotation of guilt. Of course, some attorney would quickly challenge such a designation.

In the early years of law, "absolute madness" was accepted as being a complete defense to crime if the madness existed at the time that the crime was committed. A few centuries later, it came to be accepted in the English courts that the determining condition was whether the accused was a "fool or a lunatic or a child who apparently has no knowledge of good or evil."

Next came England's famous M'Nagton case during the 1840's which involved a man who killed when his intended victim was the famous Sir Robert Peel, prime minister of England, and instead he killed a wrong man. Sir Robert had taken the precaution of having a double ride in the carriage in his stead. The attorney for M'Nagton, the accused man, contended that M'Nagton was a victim of mad delusions and was so deranged as not to have known right from wrong.

M'Nagton was acquitted and a new defense of temporary insanity had been given birth. That defense called for the attorney to show that the defendant was suffering so severely from a "defect of reason" resulting from a "disease of the mind" that he or she did not understand. The court experts concluded that a defendant who acted under an insane delusion, but was not otherwise insane, must be judged according to the facts of the offense as they seemed to him or her.

From that early foundation, the plea of temporary insanity was gradually expanded in a spiraling pattern that can best be called "lawyer creep". No matter how firmly defined the courts consider the concept of temporary insanity to be, subsequent defense attorneys have repeatedly brought forth minute extensions of the basic defense. Today's minor extension piles on the top of a minor expansion of the concept from a day earlier in an ever-broader interpretation of temporary insanity.

Finally, in the 1960's, a new version brought us up to date. The new rule calls for defendants to be judged insane and found guiltless if either of two points can be satisfactorily established in court. It must be shown that, as a result of mental distress or mental defect, the accused lacked at the time of the offense, the substantial mental capacity either (1) to appreciate the criminality (the wrongfulness) of their conduct, or (2) to conform their conduct to the requirements of the law.

The current status of that defense has resulted in a situation wherein the insanity defense may have reached it's most ridiculous acceptance. This one is particularly notable because we have the guilty man's view on the insanity defense in his own words. It has allowed Michael Levine to go unconvicted in a 1979 case in Shaker Heights, Ohio, and free to live a normal life.

Levine and an accomplice, John Files, broke into the home of Georgine and Julius Kravitz, a banker, and demanded a million dollars. Levine took the husband and wife to a motel room and was finally convinced that there was no cash available. The extortionist then ordered Kravitz into the front seat of his automobile and Mrs. Kravitz into the back seat. The intention was to travel to a number of locations to pick up smaller amounts of cash in levels that might be available.

On the way, Kravitz pointed his finger at Levine and informed him, "You had better give up." That was enough. Levine shot and killed Kravitz, then turned and shot Mrs. Levine three times. The woman managed to open the door and roll out of the moving car.

When the crime was to be prosecuted, Levine waived his right to be tried by jury and his attorney entered a plea of not guilty by reason of temporary insanity. He had a history of psychiatric problems and the act by Kravitz of pointing a finger at his captor was enough to create a condition of temporary insanity, according to his attorney. The judge accepted the claim as a proper defense.

Levine was sent to a psychiatric hospital where he was treated by a psychiatrist and almost immediately began claiming that he was cured. The doctors agreed that there was no evidence that Levine was then insane.

Levine, after the brief treatment, admitted that he was no different then than he was when he committed the crime. He said, "The whole issue of sanity or insanity is a very fluid state of mind". He was finally released from confinement and he contended that he was unjustly imprisoned for years. Every judge in the state had refused to turn him loose earlier.

The killer then formed his own corporation and hired a publicity agent. He wrote a book and summarized his case this way:

> "We are all potentially dangerous. Who knows what the future holds for any of us. I think we all have the potential to commit a homicide."

To this has the use of the temporary insanity plea evolved. The judge and juries seem certain to continue to allow the evolution to every limit. Logic can be presented that every person in America has some measure of thinking abnormalities that could be interpreted under proper circumstances as a mental disease or mental defect. It then becomes a simple matter, with all of the varied theories of how the mind works, for every defense attorney to locate a psychologist who will testify that the accused lacked at the time of the offense, the substantial mental capacity to either (1) appreciate the criminality of their conduct, or (2) conform his or her conduct to the requirements of the law.

There simply is no defining line which says that beyond this degree of insanity, the insanity defense cannot be used. Then the problem becomes one that on every jury, there will be at least one person who believes that he or she is displaying intelligence or sophistication by saying in effect that, "Yes, you other jurors may not have the same advanced understanding of the working of the mind which the psychologist is describing. I am ready to confirm the defense of temporary insanity."

That particular message may not be spoken in words but the concept is entered into the general tenor of the deliberations.

Is it not reasonable to believe that in some not too distant future, there will be acceptance of variations of the insanity defense in every crime committed in the United States, no matter how tenuous the validity of the insanity plea?

When Yale graduate Richard Herrin of White Plains, New York, was told by his girl friend, Joan Garland, 20, that she was breaking up with him, he beat her to death with a hammer. A jury qualified that message from her as "extreme mental disturbance" and so reduced his sentence to manslaughter

Everyone is familiar with the trials of Lorena Bobbit and the Menendez brothers, in both of which the "abuse excuse" was the heart of the defense. This is simply another limit in a different direction to which the insanity defense was extended. Every line in the sand can be redrawn a little further out or into a new direction. Inch by inch the limits can be extended. The problem is that there can always be a new limit established toward every point of the compass. Would it not be reasonable to expect that at some future outgrowth of this lineage, that some defense attorney would claim the first amendment as a defense, thus basing his right to kill as a matter of free speech?

In 1975, a former Detroit police officer Paul Harrington, then 29, shot and killed his wife Becky and two daughters Pamela and Cassandra. He was found innocent by reason of insanity as his attorney blamed his instability in part from his traumatic Vietnam War experiences. He spent two months in a psychiatric institution and then was freed as "Innocent for Reason of Insanity."

Twenty five years later, on October, 14, 1999, he borrowed a gun from his neighbor and on the next morning killed his wife and younger son after talking to a 911 operator for 10 minutes. A second claim of innocence by reason of insanity produced a similar result. He said that he had lost his job as a steelworker, had run out of money and medication for depression and "just couldn't handle it any more," and so decided to murder his wife and son. Again, he was found innocent by reason of insanity.

Thomas Vanda was on probation for stabbing a 13 year old girl in 1970, and was soon in jail again convicted of the stabbing death of a 17 year old girl in 1971. In 1976, a criminal court judge found him not guilty by reason of insanity in the second crime. One year later, Vanda was arrested again for the rape-murder of a 25 year old woman. This time while he was still in jail awaiting trial on the third crime, he wrote a pamphlet, "How to Beat a Murder Rap by Insanity" in which he gave detailed advice to a fellow prisoner.

In another case in 1976, a New York City policeman shot an unarmed boy at close range in front of witnesses. He first claimed that he shot the boy because the boy was reaching for a gun. But when no witnesses could be found who would verify his story, the policeman changed his plea to not guilty by reason of temporary insanity. The lawyer found a psychiatrist who would interpret the policeman's original explanation – that he shot because the boy was reaching for a gun – was a psychiatric phenomena known as "involuntary retrospective falsification". In this instance, there were enough jurors to say that "I can accept these advanced understandings of the working of the mind which..." to set the man free on the reason of temporary insanity. The man was acquitted and sent to a mental hospital. When this happened, his lawyer requested that the police department grant him a disability pension.

The juror who accepts the philosophy that – "you other jurors may not have the same learning capacity as I do but I can accept these advanced understandings of the working of the mind which the psychologist for the defense is describing. I am ready to confirm the defense of temporary insanity" – is a cancer in the cause of justice.

With no clear definition of temporary insanity, the psychiatrists can run amok. The defense can search among available psychologists to find one who is willing to declare a new basis for a theory that fits, maybe for money, maybe for the chance to announce a new theory, maybe for whatever reason.

Some states have attempted to solve the problem by passing legislation that requires the convicted felon to be sentenced to whatever sentence might be appropriate for the crime for which the person was convicted. Then, the felon is to be subjected to whatever psychiatric treatment might be deemed appropriate for the indicated mental disorder and once he has been cleared by the psychiatrist as no longer being in disorder, then the sentence shall be placed into effect and treated in all respects as the sentence justifies.

Every good and moral citizen of the United States should support laws similar to those which have been passed in those few states. Even that is only a half way step toward ridding ourselves of one of the two greatest evils in jurisprudence, maybe more so even than the three vile answers.

Chapter 20

The Right that was Inverted into an Escape Hatch

When the originators of the Bill of Rights were crafting the sixth amendment in 1791, their intention was to protect the accused person who desires a speedy trial from being forced to wait too long for the trial to which he was entitled. No definition was provided, however, for what constitutes a speedy trial. As so often happens when an issue goes before the courts, the upper courts turned what was intended to be a protection for the accused into an avenue for avoiding just punishment for crimes.

All too often, the court system has established an arbitrary deadline and with help from the defense attorney, the date of the trial can be pushed further and further away so that the case is moving closer and closer to the artificial deadline. When the state announces that it is ready for trial prior to the deadline, that should fulfill the obligation to the accused for a speedy trial. With a little maneuvering by the defense attorney, however, that proper compliance can be defeated.

Philip Connor was arrested and charged with second degree assault, then released on bail. Connor's attorney was properly informed that the state was ready for trial and a date was set when the accused should appear for trial. On the morning of the designated date, Connor appeared with his attorney. The court, however, had other business and the beginning of trial was pushed back to the afternoon.

At the set time, Connor appeared, not with his own attorney but with a partner of his regular attorney (Or did he send a different attorney to deliberately confuse the process?). They moved into the back row of the courtroom, and with a rather full courtroom, were not seen by either the judge or the bailiff. The officers for the court did not recognize the new attorney and they overlooked the fact that Connor was present. The pair departed without Connor being apprehended. He was not captured again until after the six month deadline had passed. Was Connor denied his right to a speedy trial? All charges were dropped because the beginning of the trial had missed the arbitrary deadline.

Some jurisdictions have corrected the practice of setting specific dates as the deadline to comply with "right to speedy trial". Justice will only be served when all judges are called on for a discretionary decision based on whether an accused asserted his right to a speedy trial. A further factor is that the time period must be sufficiently short that it does not in any way impair the ability of the defense to use all of its defense resources – that all witnesses are still expected to be available, that evidence will not erode or disappear, etc.

A case where that was a partial factor was the O.J. Simpson trial where the defense attorneys called for a speedy trial and the judge granted them that privilege even though the prosecuting attorneys had not had time to go through all of the evidence. This hampered the prosecution team and was a partial reason why Marcia Clark and Christopher Darden were criticized for not presenting an adequate case.

Thus, it is essential that not only must the accused be granted a beginning trial date that constitutes a speedy trial but also the judge must make a discretionary decision that the prosecution has ample time to prepare for trial.

The necessity to establish reasonably set deadlines based on the judge's discretion has been called for by any number of intelligent attorneys and seems an obvious correction to the problem.

Chapter 21

Problem Juries and Proposed Tune-ups

In all the history of the American justice system, the one problem that has probably undergone more experimentation and iteration than any other is how to determine the makeup of juries.

A very informative book, *We, The Jury* by Jeffrey Abramson, praises the jury system as "the ideal of democracy" and "one of only two exercises of pure democracy still in use in America." (The other is the town meeting). Then he provides extensive explanation of how a jury verdict is developed, not by truth as we historically understand truth, but by the weighted impact of all biases to be found in the community.

An early concept of American juries was that trials were to be decided by verdict of "twelve honest men of the neighborhood". The intent was to both limit the selection of the juries to the county in which the crime had occurred and to adopt nullification as a formal policy. The common wisdom was that jurors could ignore a judge's instructions on the law and determine the law among themselves in both criminal and civil cases.

Nullification is that circumstance that transpires when the jurors conclude that they know better what the law should be than the written law or the law as quoted to them by the judge. The jury then determines the verdict by what the members agree should be law

160

rather than the law that exists on the books. Such nullification can happen in today's trials.

Nullification has interfered with verdicts down across the centuries and is a practice that the court system has tried its best to eliminate without success. Jury nullification goes far back into English law, at least to 1670, in the famous case of William Penn being tried for illegal assembly when he had preached Quaker doctrine on the streets of London. The court had instructed the jury that such preaching was against the law but the jury refused to provide a verdict of guilty. Instead, the jurors were willing to go to prison themselves rather than accept the law as the court explained it.

Most numerous of the practices of jury nullification in the United States were, first, the trials in the North of persons who had illegally assisted runaway slaves during the years prior to the Civil War and secondly, the trials of persons in the South who were being tried for harassment or murder of Blacks during the civil rights struggle. Juries simply could not be seated who would convict the accused no matter how strong the evidence.

The practice of jury nullification continues today, the most publicized instances being the jury's refusal to convict Jack Kevorkian for violating a law that made it illegal to assist persons who wished to commit suicides.

When the Bill of Rights was adopted, it included Article VI with the clause that "In all criminal prosecutions, the accused shall enjoy the right to a speedy and public trial, by an impartial jury of the state and district wherein the crime shall have been committed, which district shall have been ascertained by law.

Steadily, an assault on jurors having advance knowledge developed. Today, instead of desiring jurors that know something about the accused, our courts view such knowledge as a threat to impartial justice. The matter of achieving impartiality has gradually come to be defined as having an empty mind. If a person has expressed an opinion on any element of the crime, then he should be disqualified. Today, jurors are treated as being so ignorant of the law that they must mechanically obey the judge's instructions to the letter.

Later, the seekers of impartial juries began to focus on pre-trial publicity. At first, trials were moved within states or districts to overcome the impact of such publicity and later it was ruled that federal trials could be moved to any other venue without regard to state limitations.

The next drive was to balance out the biases to add up to a fair representation of the strength of biases in the community. If half of the population has a certain characteristic, then an equal proportion of the jury members should ideally be of such characteristic of their makeup.

In spite of the great effort and legal craftsmanship that had gone into developing a jury that has a proportional cross section of all of the biases of the community, there is one group of biases completely missing from the model and that is the biases of the intelligent. Intelligence is the one totally disenfranchised characteristic.

College graduates are almost uniformly shunted away from jury duty mostly under the guise that their work is too crucial to be interrupted but more realistically because the attorneys don't want them on the juries, at least no graduate from one of the hard sciences – no medical doctors, no engineers, no accountants, no mathematicians, no scientists, no person who might be guilty of disciplined reasoning.

The legal specialists have for 200 years combined their best efforts to craft the balanced jury with cross-sectional participation to match identifiable blocs in proportion to their numbers. The biases of dozens of ethnic groups, nationality groups, religious groups, genders, sexual orientations, work categories, and social groups have been melded together to define a jury with which no one could be dissatisfied. Surely with so much effort entering into meeting this ideal, we should have had juries to serve the ages. So what now?

Two upsetting practices have been adopted that would ruin everything that had been created. With as much perfection as had gone into creation of Michelangelo's sculpture David, we would have thought that the juries would be considered to be perfect. But lawyers committed the equivalent of trimming those bulges of muscle and chipping away at the large feet until the perfection has been shattered. That gave lawyers the opportunity to gain advantage when needed.

The first modification was the preemptory challenge. For hundreds of years, lawyers have had the option to eliminate prospective jurors suspected of leaning to the other side. Justification was in direct contradiction of the efforts to insert the biases. In theory, these challenges are justified as a means to develop impartial juries by eliminating extremes of partiality. The legal teams may veto those jury members whom they most distrust. Preemptory challenges require no justification, no explanation, no reason except a hunch. Yet, there are still rules that the preemptory challenges must follow. In fact, the preemptory changes allow the ethos of the jury to be blown apart with a resultant total restructuring of the bias of the jury.

Obviously, the defense attorney does not have totally free range in selection of jurors but in the Timothy McVeigh case, they had 75 preemptory challenges. In the O.J. Simpson trial, each side had 20 such challenges. With a sympathetic judge who reacts favorably on causes proposed for rejection of other potential jurors, the defense attorney is often able to seat a jury very much to his or her liking, a jury that is almost handpicked. The perfect sculpture has been disassembled.

The use of preemptory challenges was accomplishing more than the court would allow because both prosecution and defense were at times using those challenges to totally eliminate Blacks. In 1986, the Supreme Court ruled that the preemptory challenges could not be used to eliminate Blacks solely for the reason of race. When one of the sides wishes to eliminate a juror on account of race, the counsel must be prepared to provide a pretended reason for expelling the juror for some other cause than race. That has led to some flimsy excuses for removing a person but the judges have been lenient on accepting any given reason.

The defense attorneys have discovered new weapons - the jury consultants. These consultants are involved in almost every trial that involves a wealthy person because they charge from $1000 to $4000 per day. The jury consultants are social scientists who have learned how to analyze people.

They may check out the bumper stickers on vehicles of prospective jurors, or they may examine the outer condition of the home of a prospect. If the individual is dressed in a disheveled manner, that suggests a favorable vote for the defense. The job history may well be the most important part of the information.

Women make better jury consultants because they have greater intuition and sensitivity. Through all of these techniques and more, these consultants can form an evaluation of the prospective juror and may well determine in advance the likelihood that a prospective candidate is likely to vote guilty or not guilty.

Jury consultants are principally used by defense lawyers and they may provide numerous contributions. First, they can identify prospective jurors who should be kept off the jury panel. They can coach the accused. William Kennedy Smith, when on trial in Miami for rape, was told to drive a family style station wagon rather than a more expensive car, was instructed in what color suit to wear in order to look innocent, and was told to change his name from "Willie" to "Will".

The profession of jury consultants has advanced so far that some jury consultants claim to have recorded 92% success rates when 90% of the accused are actually guilty. That success rate rivals some of the most expensive lawyers in America. We asserted earlier that the ability to choose, often with the assistance of the jury consultant, a jury that is predisposed toward a verdict of not guilty, is the most important step in the entire trial process. This is not justice. This is the skill, knowledge, tools, showmanship and fallacious arguments by the defense team overwhelming the truth.

Did we hear somewhere that a trial is intended to be a just determination of whether a person is guilty or innocent? Are we to believe that 92% of the accused with whom that woman was involved was a proper representation of innocence.

A proper jury and the battle is won! To hell with the truth or factual evidence.

Responsible attorneys, however, frankly admit that the jury system is in serious need of repair, even to being in a state of near collapse.

Judge Harold Rothwax described the situation:

> "Privately, they (the judges and attorneys) will acknowledge that a trial before a jury is a crapshoot...it is a comment on the procedures by which we recruit and select

jurors, and the way that we manipulate them, orient them, instruct them and condition their behavior."

Judges know that there are massive problems that are choking our jury system. Improvements are continually being proposed, not only by judges but also by dedicated lawyers. Most of these proposed changes are so logical that they have been proposed over and over by reform minded members of the bar and so are not be credited to individual lawyers.

One should not assume that extensive praise heaped on the jury system by numerous lawyers and civic leaders means that the system is a satisfactory contribution to American society. Civic leaders too often pay homage to political correctness.

A Better Jury Pool

The first and largest change that needs to be made goes not to the judges or lawyers but to the attitudes of the general public toward jury duty. I felt guilty when I had to call the jury clerk and request that my wife be excused because she was suffering from Alzheimer's disease. I didn't know then that it was the most innocuous of excuses and that almost any excuse would be acceptable. Doctors, lawyers, nurses, priests, ministers, teachers, managers, etc., are automatically released from jury duty.

Worse yet, a large percentage of the citizenry simply ignores the jury call. The practice is so common that no attempt is made to hold them accountable. For those who do appear, the judges and lawyers will then find reasons to dismiss every person who is college educated, holds a responsible work position, or takes an interest in current community or world affairs. Jurors are needed who are intelligent, educated and interested in good citizenship. Instead, the system works to bring together the stupidest and least responsible jurors who can be found.

Judge Burton S. Katz has a partial solution. He recommends that insurance companies provide policies that are to be purchased by companies or individuals. An individual is called for jury duty seldom enough that the cost should be relatively low. Companies could be required to buy that insurance for each employee whose functions need to be continued while that employee is on jury duty. When an employee is to be absent on jury duty, a temporary employment agency could be called to provide a replacement during his absence with the insurance proceeds paying for the temporary employee. If a self employed person is called, he too, might be recompensed or replaced with temporary help.

One part of the problem is the level of jury pay. A true hardship exists for some who must serve on juries at a pay scale far below their normal earnings. The jury pay scales should be equal to what is paid other well paying productive persons of the community.

We should improve the jury pool by requiring as close to a true cross section of the community as possible by stopping the current practice of releasing from the jury pool every person who has even the hint of an excuse for wanting to be excused This matter of choosing only the most stupid and bigoted people to serve on juries is so crucial that it threatens to bring down the entire jury system.

Reduce the Number of Preemptory Challenges

Second only to poor citizen participation as a crucial problem is the ability of prosecution and defense lawyers, particularly defense lawyers, to use numerous preemptory challenges to reshape a jury to their own liking. Do they want the prejudices in or out? The challenges should allow for removing persons where an ideological agenda is recognized but should be few enough to prevent a lawyer from totally rebuilding a jury to his or her liking. There should not be enough challenges to completely alter the basic makeup of the jury.

Recommendations have been offered that the number be limited to two or three challenges.

Non-unanimous Juries

The courts should allow verdicts in criminal trials that are less than unanimous.

One leading problem is the juror who has an agenda or who wants to accomplish "pay back" for some perceived injustice. This matter is even more serious as racial divisions multiply and become more intensified in this country. A juror may lie during voir dire and claim, for example, that he or she would have no problem with sentencing an accused person to capital punishment

In addition to unanimous verdicts, guilty verdicts should be achieved by an 11 to 1 vote. Some writers even recommend that 10 to 2 or 9 to 3 verdicts be acceptable. Nothing in the constitution defines any magic about a unanimous vote of 12 jurors being required for a guilty verdict. No one, however, suggests a mere majority vote.

One or two jurors can hold out against a unanimous verdict for a variety or reasons. Most injurious is the matter of the biased juror, the very individual that the system has struggled so hard to insert. Certainly, in our present society, with so many minority blocks of Blacks, Hispanics, homosexuals, Islamics, etc. feeling that they are discriminated against, this is a problem that surfaces with increasing frequency.

Judge's Instructions to the Jury

Numerous cases have been thrown out because of a higher court's displeasure with a judge's wording of instructions to the jury. They have issued so many permutations of instructions that the judges now are almost invariably afraid to issue instructions on what constitutes reasonable doubt. Consequently, they have adopted a version of those instructions that has stood the test of time and has been accepted time after time as being permissible. If a jury requests explanation of some phrase in that specific paragraph of instructions, many judges are afraid to explain for fear that their explanation will be the cause for ordering a retrial.

Even though being accepted hundreds of times on appeal, the following set of instructions on reasonable doubt is still encountering instances where it is ruled unacceptable.

"Reasonable doubt is defined as follows: It is not a mere possible or imaginary doubt; because everything relating to human affairs, and depending on moral evidence, is open to some possible or imaginary doubt. It is that state of the case which, after the entire comparison and consideration of all the evidence, leaves the minds of the jurors in that condition that they cannot say they feel an abiding conviction, to a moral certainty, of the truth of the charge."

If you, friend reader, say that you can fully understand that instruction on reasonable doubt, then you probably aren't reading it carefully. The profession has rejected the concept of morality so how can you say that you feel something to a moral certainty, and if you admit the concept, how would you define that term? What is "moral evidence?" What is "abiding conviction?"

Yet if the jury goes back to the judge for explanation on one of the terms, they are likely to be told that they have all of the instructions they are going to get and to return to the place of deliberation to fulfill the unfathomable instructions. The wording of the instruction is considered to be sacrosanct. By changing even one word or adding a bit of explanation, the defense attorneys will be almost certain to use that change as a basis for appeal. The phrase "moral certainty" was recently disapproved by a same appellate court that had previously approved it.

The logical answer to that dilemma seems to be for the judicial profession to appoint a committee and authorize it to develop a clear set of instructions written with modern day language for each term that jurors, sooner or later, will have to deal.

In a highlight of idiocy, court decisions began evolving almost as soon as the constitution was adopted whereby the judge is to inform the jury that they must, in effect, keep their brains in neutral and simply observe and listen until he gives permission to begin the processes of reason and decision making. They are not to discuss the evidence among themselves nor begin considering individually a decision of guilt or innocence until after the final arguments and instructions to the jury have been rendered. Violations of the instruction have caused numerous convictions to be remanded for retrial.

Reduce the Number of Jurors

Some specialists even recommend that a jury be reduced to 6 or 8 members. Although some state constitutions require 12 members, the federal constitution says nothing about how many should constitute a jury.

This would result in less time required for voir dire. In the O.J. Simpson case, the court required approximately 10 hours per person finally seated on the jury of 12. In most cases, it is much less but a jury of 8 would not only expedite the trial but would also save money. The time and money saved would make it possible to conduct many of the trials now ending with plea bargain because of inadequate personnel and facilities.

Bar Jury Consultants

This development in judicial proceedings is, for the most part, available only to the wealthy. The accused of lesser means cannot afford the price tag. Of course, jury consultants themselves proclaim their talents should be made available to every accused at government expense.

The principal purpose of jury consultants is to identify the likelihood of a potential juror voting guilty or innocent. Representing society's quest for fair trials seeking the truth, our goal is to keep biased prospects off of the jury panel. But the well justified desires of society are exactly the opposite of what is desired by the defense attorney and the jury consultant. They do not want the truth and they are trying to pack the jury with biased persons, the more biases the better. Jury consultants are a form of jury tampering.

Let jurors ask questions

The current rules of court procedure forbid the jurors from asking questions. This apparently stems from the illogical concept assumed by those who developed the rules that the jurors are supposed to keep their brains shut down and simply act as a recording machine until that magical moment when the case is submitted to them for decision.

The rules should be changed to allow questions from the jurors. It will be an encouraging sign if more and more questions are asked. That will make the jurors feel involved and keep them actively pursuing solutions of truth as well as keeping them from going to sleep as jurors are known to do. Many attorneys have recommended that such procedure be allowed.

But wait. Simply to allow jurors to ask questions at a time of their choosing could allow the questioner to word the question in such way that the it would be in inadmissible, i.e. "Did you hear the accused when he said that he had visited the victim that night?" Consequently, precautions would have to be taken

Judge Katz recommends that at the end of the testimony of each witness and before that witness is released, a brief recess should be declared during which time any juror or the jury as a whole could submit written questions for the witness and submit them to the judge. If the judge concurs that it is a proper question and that the answer to the question could provide further proper insights into the testimony, the judge would read the questions to the witnesses when the court is back in session and, if the question will bring forth improper responses, the judge could either clarify the question and ask the juror if that is a proper interpretation of the question, or allow the juror to submit a reworded statement of the question. Finally, if the judge refuses to ask the questions, he should explain the reason to the jury.

Let the Judge ask Questions

In England, the judges, normally a panel of three, question the witnesses. That is a logical procedure. If a judge sees an opportunity where a certain question will elicit information that will contribute to a true determination of the truth of the case, then the question should be asked and the witness should be required to answer. It does not contribute to the cause of justice to limit questioning to the prosecuting and defense attorneys.

Numerous other improvements have been described in the literature but each simply contributes a reasonable but minimum improvement to the process such as allowing jurors to talk among themselves as the trial progresses, improving physical surroundings for jurors, television cameras in the court room but giving the judge an off button to prevent prohibited shots such as pictures of the jury or close-ups of the defense counsel in discussions with the client.

Further Revolutionary Changes

The listed changes could clearly improve the jury system but they only provide moderate reform. For a more rigorous idea to achieve a cleansing revolution, the reader, along with lawyers, are invited to consider the system proposed in Chapter 24.

Part III

Top Goal – An End to the Adversarial System

The Author offers Ideas, not as Proposals, but as Concepts for Consideration and Evaluation by Members of the Bar Association

"...trials by the adversarial contest must in time go the way of the ancient trial by battle and blood." Chief Justice Warren Burger in Speech to the American Bar Association in Las Vegas, February 12, 1984

Chapter 22

Criminal Offenses and Plea Bargains

No problem on the entire legal scene is more difficult to provide a logical solution than the plea bargain. Most Americans are well aware of the evils which it can create and more people probably call for its elimination than for any other problem. It does create undesirable effects.

There had to be at least one subject on which I would change my opinion as I read more and more books on the criminal justice system. I was totally negative about plea bargains and I now consider that they can be eliminated only when most of the other problems have been resolved, particularly the matter of providing adequate infrastructure.

Lets look at the pros and cons of the plea bargain.

The pros are easy. The court system of city, county, state and federal courts are so overloaded that they need a safety valve. The plea bargain is the safety valve.

Not a small part of the problem caused by the plea bargain is the wasted time for the already overloaded police forces of the nation. 90 to 95% of all cases are plea bargained. Even the sheer numbers would totally place the court system in chaos. In Manhattan, New York City, about 125,000 cases come through arraignment court each year. In criminal court, the city has about one per cent of the capacity that would be required to handle all of the trials.

The same general situation exists in most courts throughout the land. As a second consideration, there aren't enough prosecuting attorneys to prepare all of the cases against all of the accused and do it within the time which would fulfill the accused's right to a speedy trial.

There is another situation where the plea bargain is commonly used. Frequently, if the prosecuting attorneys preparing a case have been able to develop sufficient evidence that they are certain the individual is guilty of the anticipated charge but if the evidence is not sufficiently air tight that it will meet the demands of a jury through the twists and turns entered by the defense attorney, he or she may feel justified in taking a plea bargain at a lesser charge rather than allowing the accused to go free.

Or more likely if a judge has ruled part of the evidence is inadmissible, the prosecuting attorney might decide that it is better to get a plea of guilty at a lesser charge. For example, if the judge for the preliminary trial had refused to accept the evidence developed by the four policeman when they went over the wall into O.J. Simpson's Rockingham estate without getting a search warrant, would Marcia Clark have been justified in accepting a plea of guilty to second degree murder? Or even manslaughter? Such a plea bargain would have made sure that Simpson would have been incarcerated for an extended period at a time when the thinking on the defense team seemed to be to get Simpson as small a punishment as possible. There was little thought at that point in the process that Simpson might go free. Should Marcia Clark have offered a plea bargain for second degree murder because she suspected that the defense would turn the trial into a farce with use of the race card? Yet a plea bargain would have resulted in a massive outcry from the public.

November, 2002 provided a case where the plea bargain should clearly have been used instead of a trial. Movie actress Winona Ryder, 30 years old at the time that the crime was committed, stood accused of 'Felony Theft'. She was accused of shoplifting $5500 worth of merchandise from the Saks Fifth Avenue department store in Beverly Hills. The items taken included a $1595 Gucci dress plus purses, shoes and other items. She was found guilty and sentenced to 3 years probation plus $10,000 in fines and restitution.

The Los Angeles County Court System simply does not have the capacity to process a shoplifting case in light of the overload of serious cases. We have to believe that Los Angeles County District Attorney Steve Cooley saw an opportunity to gain favorable publicity for being tough on celebrities. This may signal a future run for political office such as a congressman or governor. Actually, Prosecutor Ann Rundle gained more public recognition since she was on the television screen more that Cooley.

Investigators for the television show, "Celebrity Justice," have reported that Rundle was the assigned prosecutor on a murder trial that was postponed to make the courtroom and court personnel available for the Ryder.

The judicial justice system simply cannot accommodate substitution of the low priority trials for the serious ones no matter how it enhances the reputation of district and prosecuting attorneys. Many murder trials have been plea bargained because of the crunch of the caseload. Part of the process must be a proper setting of priorities and shoplifting simply was not as serious as murder.

Now let's examine the arguments against the use of the plea bargain.

The most serious aspect deals with the matter of record keeping on the law breaking community. We need better and more complete records of criminality as one means of slowing the tremendous problem of crime in America.

Every logical citizen agrees that having people driving on the streets and highways while under the influence of alcohol is a serious problem. The death toll on the roads from that problem is far too high. But we now look at one reason that it cannot be controlled.

The state highway patrols sponsor legislation to take those drunken drivers off the highway. The state legislatures comply with the will of the patrol and of the public and pass strict laws that could help control the problem. The governor gives total support and signs the bill. The news media proclaim the new tougher laws with approval and every resident of the state believes that the highways have been made safer. Well, almost everybody.

The city attorneys and prosecuting attorneys cancel out the impact of the tougher laws with their plea bargains. A police officer makes an arrest of a person seriously under the influence and writes up the traffic ticket to fully comply with the legal requirements. The officer takes all steps necessary to authenticate the incident. Blood alcohol samples are taken and the results confirm a level well in excess of the legal limits. After so many repeat offences, that driver's license is revoked and most are no longer able to constitute a serious hazard on the highway. Right? No.

A day or so after the incident, the ticketed driver goes and stands in a line where plea bargains are being granted. Usually, instigated by his attorney, an offer is made to plea bargain the DWI offense down to "driving 10 miles per hour over the legal speed limit" as a one point violation, to a no point "driving a defective vehicle" or some other minor violation. The judge or city attorney or other ruling authority accepts the plea to "save time and expense to the city". The drunken driving offense does not get into the driver's record but rather the lesser offense of 10 miles over the speed limit or driving an unsafe vehicle.

The attorney and the judge have thwarted the intent of the legislature, the governor and the people in their effort to take the dangerous drivers off the highway. That driver may have been arrested 10 times for DWI and yet it never shows up on his record. His license has never been put in jeopardy.

Quoting Chief Langford:

> "You can't tell that person's true record by pulling up his record. You get a bunch of stuff that never happened. You get a 'defective vehicle' charge when there was no defective vehicle. You get a DWI that's been dropped down to careless driving. That kind of stuff – bad stuff...As a result of that, we have a lot of people running out there that have a lot of different violations...that have been plea-bargained away and they just continue..."

> "As an even more serious issue, a first degree murder charge in some vicious crime is often reduced to a charge of manslaughter and the criminal is back on the streets within months. Child molestation charges are plea bargained to public nuisance charges. The list goes on and on..."

Does it have to be that way? Let's consider the matter of the traffic offenses. Again I quote Chief Langford.

"I think it would be better off if we stopped the plea bargaining and the person goes to court on whatever he has been charged with. If he is going to go to court and he actually committed the (traffic) violation, and he knows that he is going to have to face those charges, and there is a fairly good amount of evidence against him, - if he knows all that – and if he knows that there is no way to plea bargain that down, I believe most of the people would be inclined to plead guilty and save the time and expense of a trial."

A guilty plea can mean assessment of the standard fine for that offense while going to court could mean the fine plus court costs. That difference in penalty can mean a motivation to save the expense of a trial which will in turn reduce the load on the court system.

This matter of the plea bargain presents a tough question. We haven't been able to create court after court to handle the load; yet we need to have the impact of trial to convict the guilty on many crimes.

My recommendation for one improvement would be that the legal system classify every criminal charge as being subject or not subject to the plea bargains.

One potential breakdown might be:

List #1	List #2
Offense Not Eligible to be Plea Bargained Under any Circumstance	Offense Subject to being Plea Bargained at Discretion of Prosecuting Attorney
First Degree Murder	Use or Possession of Drugs
Second Degree Murder	Manslaughter
Drunken Driving	All other traffic offenses

Criminal negligence resulting in Death	Breaking and Entering
	Negligent Manslaughter
Sexual Abuse of a Child	Automobile Theft
Sale of Drugs	Larceny
Vehicular Manslaughter	Shoplifting

The deciding factor in determining whether an offense is listed on the first or second list would be whether a future repeat offender of the same offense would have a likelihood to do harm to another person. The list of offenses would need to be completed in much greater detail.

In the case of plea bargaining murder cases when the judge has refused to admit certain evidence, it would be hoped that the measures described in chapter 17 would largely solve that problem.

In the cases where the prosecution has been unable to develop adequate evidence, it is probably best that the prosecution avoid bringing murder charges to avoid the possibility of future double jeopardy defenses

The murder of Jon Benet Ramsey has presented a dilemma in such a case. There are many, including very prominent media figures who decry the failure of the district attorney to present murder charges against the girl's mother, Patsy Ramsey. Yet the prosecution knows full well that Lou Smit, a very experienced former investigator on the case, is prepared to testify that he is firmly convinced that some one else committed the murder. That testimony would weigh heavily on any jury and would undoubtedly lead to reasonable doubts. Once tried, Ms. Ramsey would be totally protected from future prosecution by that double jeopardy defense.

Should the prosecution be faulted for not attempting to plea bargain Ms. Ramsey to a second degree murder conviction and assure that she would spend a number of years in prison? Undoubtedly not, because the defense attorneys would know full well about that former investigator who would be ready to testify as a defense witness.

There is no real total answer to the problem of plea bargaining except for the state legislatures to be willing to provide greatly enlarged criminal justice facilities, both physical and with adequate qualified personnel at every level.

As a final comment, let me assure the reader that there are eminent members of the legal profession who believe that the plea bargain should be completely eliminated. I have accepted the argument that it can only be considered when many more physical facilities and human resources are added to the judicial system. Even then, the Ramsey-like case would require standing off from the plea bargains.

Chapter 23

Maximum Usage of the Best Available Resources

We have stated that Part III will be devoted to original ideas that are being submitted for consideration by lawyers. More than anything, that means eliminating the standard that the American justice system is limited to the activities by the legal profession. If other disciplines can input a contribution to make the justice system operate with more accurate and affordable results, then the services of those groups should be used.

The justice system should be an arrangement to determine the answers to questions of law with the utmost accuracy that can be achieved. It should never have been allowed to become a playing field for a single profession. The football field makes millionaires out of the performers who can pass the football with the greatest skill or with the greatest deception. The courtroom should not be intended to make millionaires out of the performers who defend their clients with the greatest skill. Nor by those with the greatest ability to deceive the system. Nor with the greatest ability to supplant truth with a version of their own choice. The courtroom is not a football field.

We can fantasize about how we would build a justice system if we would start over from scratch. We would surely begin with a learned judge to maintain a reasonable degree of control over the proceedings. We could choose whether we wanted to have the final judgment of the proceedings to be determined by a jury of peers or if we wanted to use a jury made up of trained judges to determine the truth. Or would it be a mixture of the two with peers to make the final decisions at most levels of offenses, and possibly professional jurists for cases for which lengthy or capital punishments are being requested. It would be folly to propose reconstructing a total system from the foundations established in early centuries, but it is quite reasonable to cleanse the existing system by incorporating professionals from other disciplines.

The proposals that I present in this part will largely be based on adapting the system to use psychologists and financial specialists; and to make more reasonable and effective use of paralegals. If we can persuade the citizenry to begin thinking about using the best resources available, there may be other ideas that will surface to include other disciplines.

The essence of our economic system is that the person or company who has a product or service to sell makes an agreement with the person or company who wishes to purchase that service at an agreed price. Sometimes, however, impediments exist which prevent free trade. The royal house of Windsor holds the position as the sovereign head of state because of labor agreements. Labor unions often hold the right to provide skilled labor through negotiated contracts and dole out the work assignments according to seniority. A few decades ago, big city mobs held control over certain jobs and skimmed off a portion of every paycheck. Is it a far stretch to see the lawyers holding similar control over the jobs of paralegals and, not through coercion but by licensing and through a contracted pay structure, skimming of 40 to 80% of the pay for work done by the those specialists?

The right to control over those jobs is clear enough. The lawyers got there first and, by being able to write the laws, made it a primary condition of becoming a lawyer to be a graduate of one of the law schools and to have passed an exam prepared by lawyers. That ignores the fact that the paralegals have also undergone and passed up to two years of legal course work and may have gained a great amount of knowledge about the law through decades of experience.

Obviously, the lawyers claim that the paralegals can never collect enough knowledge about the law to provide qualified services. For as long as there have been labor unions, they have been claiming that it is only through work under union rules, that a plumber or electrician can become qualified. But every employer knows there is an almost unlimited supply of non-union workers who are fully qualified to provide the same work.

That is the way it is with paralegals. The educational training of paralegals covers most of the basic law taught by law schools and they create a great reservoir of legal skills which should be available to serve the needs of the less affluent segment of society. In fact, in many law firms, the paralegals do more legal work than lawyers, the only restriction being that the pay checks must go through the lawyers who own and manage the firms. The paralegals are allowed to do essentially all legal work except for giving legal advice to a client, appearing in court and taking credit for the work. They cannot "sell" their own work or take an assignment from the client and hence cannot be paid by the client.

Many paralegal educational institutions have excellent and thorough training courses. One interviewee stated that obviously, the paralegals couldn't have been expected to absorb as much legal knowledge in two years as they would have at the great law schools of the nation. Yet the response to that could be that numerous experienced lawyers have said that they haven't used 90% of what they learned in law school. On the other hand, it is reported that 90% of what they have needed in the practice of law wasn't taught in law school.

A significant part of practicing law consists of completion of forms and the paralegals will normally have seen every form more often than the lawyers. It doesn't take much experience to know what form goes for which function and to know the intention of each line on the form.

As a common occurrence in insurance work, the paralegal normally meets with adjustors from the insurance company and negotiates compliance with the insurance contract. Then after all matters are agreed upon, the lawyer takes the final settlement to the client, the insured party, and makes a congenial presentation, explaining what a fine job the firm has done. The firm, of course, collects the paycheck and then pays the paralegal for the work at a rate far below the hourly rate charged to the client. One interviewee reported a pay scale of 1/3 to the paralegal, 1/3 to firm overhead, and 1/3 as profit to the firm partners. It should be noted, however, that junior partners and law clerks also receive similar low pay scales.

If the firm is hired to negotiate a contract, segments from previous contracts, called "boiler plate", can normally be pulled from the files and assembled into a completed document. It is seldom that a completely new statement of agreement is required and, in such cases, the paralegal is fully qualified to prepare a suitable clause. The lawyers will argue, of course, that only they have the understanding of complicated principles which might have been negotiated into the agreement but, the paralegal who has concentrated on preparing the document, will usually have a better understanding than the lawyer who has attended civic meetings, entertained potential clients, and will represent the client in court.

If it is a real estate contract, the paralegal probably does 100% of the firm's work in the field and is better informed on current practices than the person for whom he or she works.

A common practice that the paralegals can properly perform is the work for people with Medicare problems. The paralegal is fully qualified to spend the necessary hours screaming at the government processors about the meaning of a clause regarding improper charges, improper payments, etc. Then the attorney calls the client in and explains what wonderful things "we" did to get reimbursements or lower fees.

Having negotiated huge contracts myself, I know that the personality and insights of the negotiator are more important than the legal knowledge. The negotiator must be prompt to recognize nuances in wording and, more importantly, to recognize potential ambiguities. Full command of the English language is more important than knowledge of contract law.

I remember one incident when our firm was preparing to issue two requests for bids in accordance with government regulations. This essentially amounted to tentative contracts and contracts, to meet all regulations, might involve a stack of paperwork up to half inch thick.

It was suggested that to meet the deadlines, I would prepare one of the contracts, and our staff lawyer would prepare the other. As part of the formality of complying with the government structure, our requests would be forwarded to higher level legal offices for review before being approved for issuance. When the documents were returned to us from the reviewing office for correction and issuance, my request had two one-phrase corrections that were to be corrected. Pages prepared by the staff lawyer were seas of red. Each page averaged about a dozen corrections, some very extensive.

The staff lawyer had the formal qualifications to be a qualified member of the bar. My training was roughly similar to an experienced paralegal but I did that work on a repetitive basis.

In another incident, my son-in-law, Richard Guarneros and a friend Jerry Petoia decided that they wanted to form a corporation. They requested that I join their Board of Directors and asked if I could prepare the papers needed for incorporation. I did as requested but also called a meeting of all principals so that I could explain the precise legal implications of being incorporated. When he heard the explanation of the ramifications of being incorporated, my son-in-law retreated and the idea collapsed.

Later, Petoia decided that he wanted to incorporate alone and requested my permission to use the papers that I had prepared. He would merely change names, purpose and specifics as required. Without having reason to have confidence in me, he submitted the package to a lawyer for review. When they came back to him, the lawyer had changed one word as "but" became "and". Non-lawyers can easily learn to do much of the work which lawyers would claim only they can perform.

The principal areas where paralegals could concentrate most effectively would be in the fields of Administrative, Agency and Contract Law. They should be required to stay out of areas likely to result in litigation or cases which might start out as a matter for one specialty and over the lifetime of the case, gravitate into the domain of another. That could require careful definition of areas of contract law which might be permissible, or careful recognition by the paralegals of what would be allowable.

There are a few unbiased attorneys who will agree that the paralegals could do most of the work required by the lower income population. Reasonable qualifications should be set down based more on years of work than on formal classroom requirements intended to protect the jobs and the income of the lawyers. The paralegals should be able to open their own office and receive pay for their work. It would probably be logical to permit approvals to be required in each specialty before that one could be practiced. Legal training courses, at the formal law schools as well as at community colleges, should be molded to fit the education truly needed.

When working for a law firm, the paralegals should be paid at a rate commensurate to the work that they actually perform and a reasonable portion of the pay that the firm receives from the client for the work.

This would be a great step forward in utilization of the best resources available. Most importantly, that could provide much of the legal capability that the lower income people need at reasonable cost. This would serve the group that is so ill served by the legal profession.

Chapter 24

Introduction of the Court Interrogator

Former Chief Justice of the Supreme Court, Warren Burger confirmed what we all know:

"Trials by the adversarial contest must in time go the way of the ancient trial by battle and blood.".

Numerous American lawyers have written that the adversarial system is a major contributor to today's sorry state of criminal justice. The adversarial system is simply not consistent with ideals of justice. Many attorneys condemn a court of justice as a lottery.

In an intelligent American society, the continued deterioration and the improper conduct of lawyers cannot go on forever. When the adversarial system will be discarded, no one can predict. A decade? A half century? Full century?

If various attorneys have blamed the culture within the profession and have foreseen the end of the adversarial system, none that I have located have written with any hint or hope of any kind of revolutionary system that should follow a discard of the existing system. A suspicion surfaces that in the law schools, the students are so thoroughly indoctrinated to revere and believe in the adversarial system that every graduate has a closed mind toward even thinking about what could replace it

Let us tread with daring and boldness in footsteps where lawyers have seemingly been reluctant to travel. If we throw conceptual crumbs upon the waters, maybe they will germinate and provide the basis for an honorable and effective justice system. If we can but initiate exchanges of ideas on what should replace the adversarial system, we will have served a worthy purpose.

With Part III being dedicated to providing ideas for lawyers to consider, the first principle must always be to utilize the best available resources. That means acknowledging that the American justice system is not a private possession of the lawyers but that it belongs to the total American people.

Lawyers would argue that all that is needed is to clean up abuses to return to a reasonable and proper system. The idea of combat between adversaries seems such a noble strife.

Attorney Lloyd Paul Stryker summarized as follows:

"A trial is still ordeal by battle. For the broadsword, there is the weight of evidence; for the battle axe, the force of logic: for the sharp spear, the blazing gleam of truth; for the rapier, the quick and flashing knife of wit."

How poetic but how inadequate for determining truth in a court of justice!

I would argue that the legal community has had almost a thousand years of evolution from the days of trial by combat and, beginning at some unidentified turning point, development of the adversarial system has been on the down slope away from any advanced state of perfection.

American Jurist Irving Kaufman stated that:

"The institution of trial by jury is over 1000 years old. But it may not last another 50 unless we can show the American public that it is an efficient tool for the administration of justice."

The science of chemistry began as alchemy probably around the 4th century B.C. as practitioners attempted to turn copper and lead into gold and silver. Over the centuries, chemistry rose from one that postulated that there were four elements - fire, air, water, and earth - and developed into a highly sophisticated field of study which identifies and can isolate approximately 118 elements, endless isotopes and millions of compounds. They can then cause them to be transformed from one into another. That represented an incredible expansion of knowledge and a willingness to change basic principles as new information became available.

Electrical engineers have moved from the study of lightning to the use of electricity for every kind of control and labor saving device that can be imagined.

The field of medicine probably began in prehistoric times with making a hole in the skull to allow the evil presence to escape from the victim. Certain practices were eliminated and others were added repeatedly until medicine today is totally different from what it was in its early days. Heart transplants, chemotherapy, kidney dialysis, limb replacement, brain surgery, elimination of infantile paralysis, immunization against typhoid and small pox all stand as symbols of the advancement of medical science.

Engineering has gone from building narrow roads and simple bridges to interplanetary space travel, underwater travel, sophisticated home appliances, high speed automobiles, ships and every conceivable machine for an improved standard of living.

Almost every field of human endeavor has recorded phenomenal advancements during the great eras of learning. But what of the legal profession's trial procedures? Can lawyers claim that it has accomplished anything in those same centuries except that it has held tight to the adversary system through good times and bad, and merely made slight changes in form? Have they achieved a higher percentage of correct and just verdicts than what occurred 400 years ago? The everlasting judgment of the lawyers is that "Justice has been served."

If the profession is genuinely interested in improving the criminal justice system, the logical step is to turn to the field of psychology, a profession that was recognized as a scientific study in the 19th century. That was many centuries after the adversarial system was entrenched as the foundation of trial law.

Psychology, according to the dictionaries, is the science of mental processes and behavior. Where are mental processes more involved than in trial law? The lawyers should long ago have folded the skills of the psychologist into a more integral part of the trial process

Presentation of this concept presupposes that the real purpose of trials is to develop truth, total truth and not the lawyer's normal goal of truth shaped by false influences, shaded by biased jurors, or occurrences during the trial.

The mind is the depository of memories. The science of psychology is the study of the working of the mind. Who better than the psychologist to draw accurate responses from the mind and cause the respondent to frame the data into useable information?

Since psychologists are the scientists who deal with processes of the mind, and since the answers to all questions, in a trial or elsewhere, develop in the mind, it follows that the psychologist should be the scientist most able to develop relevant and truthful answers.

Basically this proposal would involve a new profession, a new highly trained and skilled questioner of potential jurors and later as interrogator of witnesses as they deliver testimony to the court. During voir dire questioning, the basic purpose is to investigate the attitudes and suitability of a potential juror to serve as such. The root part of that process should be to explore how the potential juror thinks and what impact various influences will have on his thinking process. The lawyer is expected to know the law but it is the trained psychologist who knows the process of thought.

Even more important than voir dire, the questioning of witnesses under oath could best be performed by a trained psychologist. The proposal would then be to take a group of carefully selected psychologists and provide special training where they would become interrogators in the court room.

As a first look at a more effective system, we begin by following another common procedure. As soon as a judge is appointed by the supervising criminal court judge, or whomever has that responsibility, to be the presiding judge in the case to be tried, the supervising trial interrogator would appoint one of the trained interrogators to be a "Psychologist of the Court" although it probably would be preferable that this person be referred to as "Interrogator of the Court". This person would have a responsibility to be impartial equal to that of the trial judge.

The interrogator would be an officer of the court and would be paid in the same manner as the judge. However, it is logical that the length of questioning would be greatly shortened, thus, reducing the overall cost of the trial.

Continuing a review of how such a system might work, the prosecuting attorney, with an admittedly reduced role, would have full responsibility for managing the trial, for making an opening statement, for deciding what evidence is to be presented for the prosecution, for deciding which witnesses will testify about each piece of evidence, for deciding when evidence is to be withdrawn, and for scheduling the various actions.

The prosecuting attorney would begin by calling a first witness, establish identification of the witness and state what testimony will mean to the trial and then turn the witness over to the interrogator. The interrogator would then question the witness with equal responsibility to identify false testimony as well as to establish the veracity of confirming testimony. When the interrogator concludes that he has developed an accurate version of what the witness knows, the witness would then be turned over to prosecutor and defense attorney in turn with each having an opportunity to bring the witness's testimony closer to the desired meaning according to his or her desires.

There is more that the Interrogator of the Court could accomplish than the mere questioning of witnesses. During Voir Dire, the Interrogator would explore the attitudes of potential jurors. Whether the Interrogator takes a passive role and merely develops the information to enable the judge to make the decision on each potential witness or whether he would make recommendations on which should be seated and which should be rejected could best be determined by experience.

University psychologists would be required to shape the educational requirements for training future interrogators and to define which psychological concepts should be most powerful in seeking truth. Their goal would be to identify patterns of questions for use in the courtrooms. The end goal would be to develop a curriculum of study that would train psychologists to be a part of the judicial process and to become skilled questioners of witnesses.

The ultimate goal of this or subsequent proceedings would be to develop qualifications for a Registered Professional Court Interrogator – an RPCI. The standards to become an RPCI should be as rigid and as demanding as the bar examinations which finalize the acceptance of lawyers.

The RPCIs should hopefully be the best that the field of psychology has to offer, and would, like the judge, be fully accredited officers of the court. We accept the assumption that the judge is impartial and we should be equally able to accept the Registered Professional Trial Interrogator as being impartial. Would this mean that every witness in the courtroom is to be questioned by these specially trained interrogators? This is an answer that would evolve as the new standards are put into practice.

It appears highly likely that there is at least one class of witness where the presiding judge would make the decision to turn the witness over to a prosecuting attorney or a defense attorney. That would be the hostile or recalcitrant witness, the one who clearly has pertinent knowledge of the relevant matters at issue and who appears to be determined to hide that information from the court. At this early stage of proposing the practice, I would neither declare a requirement that the witness be interrogated solely by an official interrogator or by a prosecuting or defense attorney. Most probably the best practice will turn out to be first questioning under the sympathetic approach of the Interrogator followed by a rougher question session by the Prosecuting Attorney or the Defense Attorney.

The jurors would then be able to witness how the individual answers questions under a truth seeking person, and then how that person answers questions in a hostile environment while responding to a lawyer who is seeking answers to serve his own purposes. Surely, the time when the Interrogator would be most productive is for that great preponderance of witnesses who are neither hostile nor friendly to the accused but are rather witnesses who possess some information that is vital to the case, who wish to contribute their information as good citizens, and who will be most productive as witnesses in an environment that they can trust to be interested simply in evoking the truth.

Let's examine a few incidents from that case of all cases, the case of the century, and one with which every American is most familiar - the trial of O.J. Simpson for murdering Nicole Brown Simpson and Ronald Goldman.

We begin with Allen Parks, the limousine driver, who was once called an ideal witness because he was offering his testimony purely in the interest of justice and wanted to be helpful to the cause of truth. He had a good vocabulary and could express himself in a totally lucid manner. Still, in his time on the witness stand in the first Simpson trial, two erroneous results occurred which may have had a significant bearing on the decision by the jurors. We are not unmindful that a jury had been seated which was most likely to acquit Simpson but still that jury was apparently looking for excuses to present a "not guilty" decision.

The most crucial misunderstanding which could have been cleared up by a trained psychologist was probably Parks failure to be clear on the spot where he first saw Simpson. In the first trial when questioned by Marcia Clark, he had been asked to identify that spot and his means of identifying it was to give directions to a technical aide who was operating a telestrator to mark the spot. The matter of which side of the driveway would later turn out to be crucial and Allen Parks did not appreciate that fact. In directing the telestrator operator, he said, "Move it, move it, move it," until he had the X the right distance from the gate but on the wrong side of the driveway. Then he said, "Okay, there." Thus the telestrator operator had placed an "X" among some benches instead of on the opposite side of the driveway near the parked Bentley where Parks actually saw Simpson first. Parks later confirmed the improper placement under oath in the civil trial.

This may or may not have made enough difference but it was the one bit of testimony that the jurors requested be reread while a single juror had not yet surrendered to the majority, and almost immediately thereafter, the jury came in with a finding of "not guilty". Had a psychologist been asking the questions, is it not much more likely that he or she would have sensed the error as Parks caved in to the defense attorney on placement of the "X"?

In a second error that was created with Parks on the stand, he had testified that when he saw Simpson cross that driveway, he was wearing "all dark clothing, dark pants, dark top". It became necessary for Johnny Cochran, the leading defense antagonist to rebut that testimony and the defense came up with a revised scenario. Cochran posed the "corrected" version that Simpson came out of the house with a flowing "hem of a robe, swirling around". He asked in an intimidating manner if it could not have been such a robe that Allen Parks saw instead of what he had testified, and Parks, wanting to be agreeable, accepted the new version to avoid being hassled by Cochran. That dark sweat suit was essential to the flow of events and Parks' meek acceptance of different clothing opened the door still further. A trained psychologist could have avoided that trap.

Dennis Fung, the criminalist who collected all of the blood evidence was similar to Allen Parks in that "he just wanted to get along" and was not of a nature to stand up and say "that isn't the way it was" whenever Johnny Cochran proposed a revised version of events or circumstances.

If Allen Parks was a good example of a situation where a psychologist would benefit the judicial process, Dennis Fung was the better example. Fung was a competent criminalist. After interviewing him, one lawyer described him, thus. "Dennis Fung was a sweet man, a great man, but a sitting duck for any kind of clever cross-examination." Another said, "Fung was naïve and totally guileless…He will not even try to figure out where you are going with a question…He is easily led and is fully capable of saying things that he does not mean."

Barry Scheck would ask questions like, "Do you agree that it was a mistake to put a blanket on the victim's body." Fung would answer, "Yes, it was a mistake." Then, "you agree that it was a terrible mistake." "Yes, it was a terrible mistake." But in fact there was no reason to call it a mistake at all, and it certainly had no bearing on the case. Also, Fung didn't seem to understand the difference between the word "I" and "We" and tended to intermingle the two words.

Yet there was no evidence that it had in fact caused any mistake or problem. By the time Fung had confessed to innumerable mistakes which were really of no significance, the defense was able to make "blood contamination" a rallying cry which was spoken over and over as though that was the point on which the entire prosecution case fell apart. In fact, the blood collection and handling had been performed in a workmanlike manner with only a single error of significance. A rusty nail on the white back fence at Bundy had been circled and the attempt made to lift it as blood evidence had been fruitless. But that insignificant error had no bearing on the overall case.

So if Allen Parks was a good example and Dennis Fung was a better example of a witness who could have provided better testimony if questioned by a psychologist, Kato Kaelin was the ultimate example. Kato's problem was that he could not speak normal decipherable English. Instead, his talk was branded as "Californiaspeak", a mix of beach slang, partial sentences, and gestures. There is good reason to believe that Kaelin was trying his best to give truthful evidence as needed for the prosecution case,

"Kato, in fact, speaks Katospeak". He did not build his sentences around nouns and verbs but simply threw out ideas in short bursts of words which if carefully examined, had a complete thought buried somewhere in the mishmash.

Kato Kaelin turned down a million dollars from the tabloids and he appears to have been a genuine friend, loyal to Nicole, with a full interest in assisting the prosecution. But with Marcia Clark's lack of adequate time to probe Kaelin's adventurous speech, she came to consider that he was a hostile witness and requested that Judge Ito declare him as such. If ever a psychologist was needed to prompt a witness to provide useable testimony, it was in the case of Kato Kaelin.

We have said that the purpose here would be to revolutionize courtroom procedure. And so it must. The new procedures will have to be forced on the legal profession because it is in the best interest of the total American people and will begin to restore respect for the court system.

Clearly the Registered Professional Court Interrogators would reduce the role of the Prosecuting Attorney and particularly of the

Defense Attorney, but the one that would benefit most would be the lady holding the scales of justice. Yet we have little hope that it will be accepted except after much dialog by the public and by those who pursue public office.

The Court Interrogator would question the witness about the evidence with the sole goal of evoking truth from the witness. The witness would now be able to testify under sympathetic questioning by a skilled individual who is judged to have no partiality for either the claims of the prosecution or the defense. Truth would be the objective.

We necessarily accept the assumption that the judge has no partiality toward either the prosecution or for the defense and there is no reason that we cannot accept an assumption that the trial psychologist is equally void of bias.

The jury would be able to listen to testimony brought forth by an unbiased questioner and this testimony would normally have far more credibility in determining guilt or innocence than that developed under hostile questioning. It would ease the burden on the jury members.

The defense attorney or the prosecuting attorney would have the right to object to specific questions or to a line of questioning with the judge making the decision whether that line should be continued. If revisions to procedure proposed in this chapter are instituted, this consideration could become irrelevant.

Once the trial interrogator has completed his or her questions to the witness, that witness would be turned over to the defense attorney for further questioning. Certainly, the defense attorney would try to cast doubt on unfavorable testimony but the jury would be able to see the reaction of the witness under both types of treatment. The RPTI might well be called to renew questioning in a manner that would clarify anything that was brought out by intimidation or poorly asked questions.

The judge would at all times have the option of returning the witness to the trial interrogator. The judge would likewise have the authority to terminate questioning that is unduly hostile or that attacks the character of the witness when it is not justified.

In the end, guilt or innocence would, of course, be decided by a jury.

Obviously, I cannot have concocted a total complete pattern that covers every aspect of the system. The existing jury system took almost 1000 years to evolve and my proposed system would also need evolution. I said, however, that we need to use the best resources available and the Trial Interrogator would provide a big step forward in criminal justice.

Chapter 25

Introduction of the Financial Consultant

I have never been in a jury room when the jurors are determining the size of a liability award. Nor have I discussed the topic with any jurors who have been required to perform such a duty. Yet, I don't need to have those experiences to recognize one resource that could beneficially be added to the tort trial system.

Most jury panels simply do not have the resources either in knowledge or in suitable instructions to establish financial amounts on any rational basis. Where dollars and time are both involved, financial amounts cannot be calculated with out a working knowledge of compound interest and lawyers for the plaintiffs have taken full precautions to keep all persons who would understand that complex subject off the jury panel. Probably 95% of high school graduates lack the proper understanding to calculate a logical amount for a financial award. Lawyers may have understood compound interest only as it applies to their own massive investments.

In a pure compound interest problem, the jury wants to award a plaintiff $5000 per month for 50 years. An annuity, at 5% annual interest compounded monthly, can be purchased. What amount of award will provide these benefits?

The required jury award would not be three million dollars, as some would calculate, but $907,566. A one million dollar award would be more appropriate than three million.

Our students have by and large been playing video games or attending movies or watching the television wasteland when they should have learning the cause and effects of compound interest. And it isn't only the students. A survey of adults would disclose that 90%, the very pool from whom jurors are drawn, do not understand the concepts. So I know that knowledge is not a factor in the jury deliberation rooms.

At the beginning of each judicial term, each judge should have been supplied with a list of qualified people appointed to serve as "financial consultants to the court". These individuals shall have been qualified as financial consultants through experience and training either as accountants, bankers, financial advisors, or as mathematicians or any of a variety of occupations which understand the meaning of financial numbers with a consideration of time. One such consultant should be kept available whenever a jury may be considering punitive damages

The instructions to the jury in a damage suit should tell the jurors not to try to calculate the amount of the damage award but instead to compile a list of benefits that are to be provided for a victim. Then the jury should, in addition to informing the judge that a proper verdict has been reached, include notice that an appropriate list of benefits has been agreed to. The judge would direct a financial consultant who is an officer of the court to go into the deliberation room to convert the list of desired benefits into an approximate amount of the final financial award. The financial consultant should logically be working from a set of guidelines previously printed and approved by the court

The list would of course, be based on the jury's knowledge of the physical condition of the victim or other harmful impact on the victim. For example, a typical list of intended benefits might include:

1. A fixed income of $4000 every month for life with an annual increase of 6 per cent.
2. A motorized chair capable of traveling a 10 mile radius (with provision that it be replaced every three years)
3. An allowance for five years of college tuition

4. An allowance for a daily visit from a visiting nurse to assist with such personal care as bathing
5. A weekly visit with a psychiatrist for a period of three years.

If, instead of mere damage awards, we are looking at punitive damages, I have already argued that they have no place in a lawsuit except as a sop to the lawyer's greed. This proposed addition of the financial consultant as an additional resource is intended to eliminate certain biases which should not have a proper role in determination of damage awards. Typical biases might be:

- A sympathy for the victim which has created a desire to be generous
- A lack of understanding of the time value of money
- A bias against corporations in general
- A bias against insurance companies in particular
- A desire to punish the party deemed to be the perpetrator
- Improper influence of the plaintiff's lawyer based on his desire to add to his personal wealth

The general public is ready to condemn jury awards based on too much impact from these forces. The financial consultant would then be the one charged with converting that intended list of benefits into a reasonable damage award.

This procedure could reduce the amount of the total jury awards to about one third of the present total awards. This would reduce the cost of insurance to the insurance buying public and thus would benefit all of society.

Part IV

Solutions Needed for Overloaded Systems

Solutions are desperately needed, but no serious proposals are even being considered. The legal profession needs a push from the non-lawyering public.

Chapter 26

The News Media are Part of the Problem

Members of the news media would rather distribute sensational stories to the public than contribute to a fair and just trial. There are several negative impacts which the news media makes when interfering with our system of justice. Fortunately, famed lawyer Gary Spence, filling a role of part time journalist himself, has dissected the impact on that greatest of all prototypes, the O.J. Simpson trial. He did that, along with examining other interferences, in his book, *The Last Word*.

We have tried to be convincing on the point that to lawyers, an accurate verdict is not important but rather it is crucial that the verdict be achieved according to oft times misguided rules. To the journalists, it is not an accurate verdict that is important but ratings. How many newspapers can they sell? How large an audience can the trial events, truth or fiction, attract?

Dozens of commentators, some of them experienced lawyers and law professors, ignored any presumption of innocence. Indeed, O.J.'s conduct including disappearance while carrying $10,000 in cash and then being followed by the freeway chase all gave good reason to believe that he was guilty. In fact, there is no legal requirement for a presumption of innocence except in pre-trial or trial procedure, but one would have thought that the lawyers would have avoided that conclusion to keep from influencing the potential jury pool.

Soon after the investigation began, the police chief of Los Angeles requested that the media not attempt to interview witnesses because it might "delay and negatively impact the investigation". First, the media did not publicize that announcement and then they treated it as an invitation to interfere even more. Surely, the police were hiding something from the "people's right to know".

That "people's right to know" came from misguided Supreme Court Decisions over the centuries and has about as much validity as the court issued Exclusionary Rule. It should be wiped off the books as an inviolable rule of law.

The media has been empowered to expose injustice and corruption but that does not justify making a mockery of the justice system. Spence concludes that,

> "if the decision comes down to whether someone gets a fair trial or whether the media gets a story that renders a fair trial impossible, the results are predictable".

Court officials went through the sham that they were helping to achieve a fair trial by sequestering the jury. As the trial wore on, the defense attorneys gave daily news conferences and planted stories that would render a fair trial impossible. They knew that in spite of the sequester, the information would reach the jurors in their hotel rooms either by conjugal visits or through violation of the rules of sequestration.

In an early version of New Yorker magazine, reporter Jeff Toobin laid out a plan on how the defense strategy should play the race card to negate the impact of Officer Mark Fuhrman's discovery of the glove behind Simpson's guest house. The media was not reporting the news. It was helping to plan the defense.

If that trial is, in any sense, to be considered to be a fair test of the American justice system, then the matter of Jill Shively may very well have been the deciding point in the entire trial, the one where a different decision by the prosecutor would surely have swung the verdict to guilty. On June 14, the night of the crime, Shively had made a late evening trip to a salad bar on San Vicente Boulevard. The time was 10:45 on the night of the murder.

Driving eastward on San Vicente Blvd., Shively increased speed to get through a changing light. Simultaneously, a white Ford Bronco was driving north on Bundy in a rush that was ignoring the light. Both vehicles slammed on their brakes so that both came to a stop with the Bronco resting partially up on the raised median. Almost immediately, another vehicle headed in the opposite direction to Shively slid to a stop to avoid piling into the two stopped cars.

For seconds, the three drivers glared at each other from a few feet apart. Soon the driver of the Bronco began honking his horn and yelled, "Move that damn car." Immediately, noticing that the driver in the white Bronco looked familiar, Shively recognized that the voice was that of O.J. Simpson, a voice that she had heard so often on television. She copied down the license number of the Bronco as it backed out of the congested corner. Later, she reported to the police that the tag number was 3CZW788.

The next morning her mother informed her that Nicole Simpson had been murdered and Shively soon related the events of the night before to the police along with the tag number of the offending Bronco. That vehicle, the police soon confirmed, belonged to Simpson. Soon she was subpoenaed to appear before the grand jury investigating the Nicole Simpson murder. Unfortunately, her name was leaked to the media and immediately the interfering press was after her. On the day before she was to appear before the grand jury, she gave an interview to the producers for the television show, "Hard Copy". For that interview, the hard working mother with bills due was paid $5000.

Shively's testimony, particularly as reinforced by the license number of Simpson's Bronco, should have been the pivotal evidence. She had made a positive identification of Simpson and had given an accurate license plate report. That would have placed Simpson on the route home from the site of the murders at almost the precise time that would have established an accurate time line for the murder. It would have proven Simpson's claim of chipping golf balls in his back yard to be a lie. Or that he was sleeping as he testified. Or that he was taking a shower. That was as close to an eyewitness as the prosecution was ever going to get.

The one problem was that she had been paid $5000 for the interview. Defense attorneys were certain to claim that she had made up the story in order to collect $5000. Marcia Clark, the prosecuting attorney, made the decision to keep Shively's story under wraps and not to allow the jury hear it. It isn't illegal for a witness to be paid to divulge their pending testimony but it is certainly looked on with disfavor by court officials. Undoubtedly, that was Marcia's biggest mistake of the trial.

Marcia apparently was convinced that this was a case of spousal abuse carried to it's most terrible extreme, a throat slashing murder. Instead of using Shively's substantiated evidence, she placed on the stand Faye Resnick who had written a book, *"Nicole Brown Simpson: The Private Diary of a Life Interrupted"* and had received more than four million dollars for it. Why was it indefensible that Shively had been paid $5000 and not that Resnick had received four million dollars? Marcia did not hesitate to put the high paid Resnick on the stand to describe the developing abuse but she bypassed the recipient of a much smaller sum of money. The book by an admitted recovering drug addict, created a sensation and instead of the judge's admonishments for the jury to avoid reading the book, the jurors unquestionably made sure that they did exactly that. The book unquestionably tied together much of the other evidence but the Shively evidence could have done more than that.

The media, this time represented by Hard Copy, had eliminated the last vestige of a fair trial. The best evidence had flown on the wings of clouds.

I, like everyone else, watched most of the trial and saw the evidence and testimony as they were laid out before the jury, but it took Gary Spence to explain how totally, the actions of the news media destroyed any semblance of a fair trial.

Let's look at another abysmal example of conduct of the news media. In the remote mountains of Montana, Kari Swenson, an Olympic biathlete, was on a lakeside training run when she was kidnapped by a father-son pair. The older man, Don Nichols, had a dream of establishing a tribe of mountain people who would live deep in the uninhabited regions of Montana. To establish such a tribe, he needed a woman for breeding purposes to mate with his son Dan. The blonde jogger was the dream specimen. Captured and dragged over the mountain trails while chained to one of the men, Keri was desperate.

Search parties finally located the pair at a campsite, and in the rescue effort that followed, one of the rescuers was slain. Many interviews with psychologists preceded the trial for kidnapping and murder.

The news media from the surrounding mountain region began treating the story as though it was a tale of romance from the old West. How chivalrous that Dan would kidnap a young blonde athlete to be a future queen of his castle. Right out of the tales from medieval times! Some traveling armored knight would not have hesitated to capture a beautiful maiden that he found in the forest.

Never mind that young Dan was a convicted murderer. During his father's trial, he was roaming the courthouse modeling the latest western fashions, signing autographs, and charging a fee to pose for photographs with family groups.

Some media persons could not understand why the family and relatives were upset with the development. The book *"Victims - The Kari Swenson Story"* was written by the athlete's mother Janet Milek Swenson.

Chapter 27

Two Crises at Our Doorstep

Our children face two crises that are developing all too rapidly. One involves the upwardly spiraling amount of litigation brought on in part by the rapid increase in the number of lawyers. The second crisis involves the steadily increasing number of criminals at loose in our society. This one is being instigated by the hypocritical actions of our lawmakers.

The unfortunate fact is that a very easy method has been created whereby every lawyer can easily become wealthy at the expense of the non-lawyers and particularly the poor. That depends on the willingness of the lawyer to turn to class-action lawsuits, liability lawsuits, corporate lawsuits, defense of wealthy clients against criminal charges, and handling divorce settlements for those same wealthy persons

If, however, he or she wishes to focus on practicing law for the good of mankind by helping people with their passage through the back roads of daily life, i.e., preparing wills, deeds and trusts, contracts for individuals, researching property rights for individuals, sorting out royalties, document drafting, handling divorces or probates for the poor and middle classes or helping the indigent and downtrodden in their bouts with the law, the lawyer will remain for life in a modest economic status. In fact, he will be one of the victims of his more avaricious brethren.

The numbers tell the story. In 1960 there were 286,000 lawyers practicing in the United States. Today, that number has grown to over a million.

One Million Lawyers

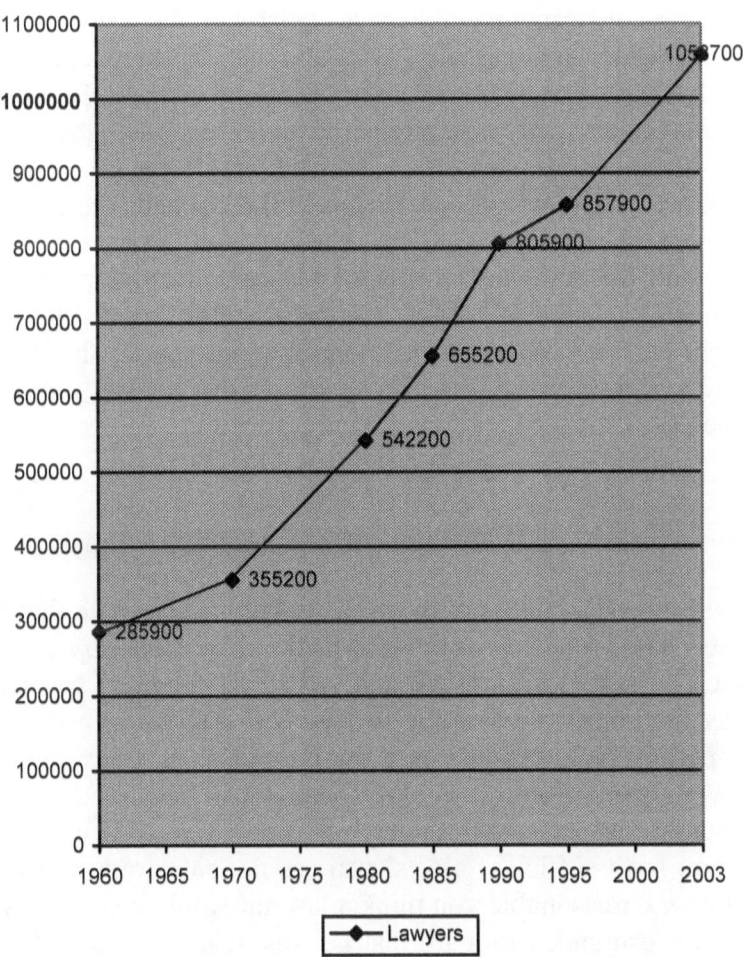

Number of Practicing Lawyers in the United States
(Courtesy of The American Bar Association)

Those attorneys who represent most of the increases didn't get into the profession to dwell among those who sought to help mankind.

If the young lawyer wants to become a quick millionaire, the path lies through the big ticket actions of liability lawsuits or class action lawsuits against the doctors, lawyers, (yes, lawyers) and corporations. How high are the rewards? Joe Jamail collected 950 million dollars, most of it from a single lawsuit in which Pennzoil sued Texaco into bankruptcy.

In the records, innumerable cases exist where lawsuits have been filed both where the defending party did not believe it could happen and with illogical end results. Take Ida Weitz of Victoria, Texas. In a moment of generosity, she purchased an automobile which she gave to her Marine son who was stationed at Camp Lejeune, North Carolina. A friend of her son borrowed the car and was involved in an accident. The driver, a Marine, was not likely to have much more money than the son, now owner of the car. Deeper pockets were needed so the lawyer for an accident victim sued Mrs. Weitz, although she no longer had an ownership interest in the car. The claim was made that she should have known that her son was likely to loan the car to some friend who was irresponsible.

— ∎ — ∎ — ∎ — ∎ — ∎ — ∎ — ∎ — ∎ — ∎ —

Exploding Number of Massive Damage Awards

I will not rely solely on my own file but am fortunate that Walter K. Olson has written two excellent books, *The Litigation Explosion*, in which he makes a thorough analysis of the litigious problems, of the way the courts are reacting to law suits and the remedies which can hopefully be applied to ease the problems. The lawsuit against Mrs. Weitz came from his book. Those books have made my task a lot easier because he covers so much of what I wanted to cover.

If you have sufficient assets, you are not safe from a lawsuit no matter how unreasonable you think a lawsuit would be. A New York doctor was astounded to learn that he was being sued for $5 million on a childbirth on which he had assisted 21 years earlier. The suit charged that improper handling of the delivery had caused a birth defect. The child, now a young man of 21, had truly suffered brain damage but how could any doctor remember the details of that long ago procedure. Yet no one could provide a clue as to what had gone wrong. The named doctor had not even been the obstetrician. Rather, he had merely assisted in the delivery and the doctor who had actually delivered the baby was dead. The lawyers had dredged up the records and had filed suits against every member of the team that had delivered the child

Until 1978, lawyers were generally forbidden to advertise or even to seek clients. It is true that the ban was not totally effective as the lawyers found ways to fish for business while only marginally ignoring the rules. First, there was a decision that druggists could not be denied the opportunity to advertise for business. Under the guise of reform, more and more professions were allowed to advertise and the general opinion among lawyers could be summed up by asking how much more legal business could be generated if lawyers were allowed to advertise. Then came a sequence of court decisions which set in motion a great nationwide deluge of lawsuits.

Within one year a law firm began advertising four kinds of routine legal work – adoptions, name changes, uncontested divorces, and bankruptcies where there had been a pleading of "no contest". Within a month, the dam broke and lawyers began advertising all types of legal work except liability lawsuits in every state in the union. First tentative efforts at advertising for clients with potential injury lawsuits worked so well that the practice exploded. Payments for television advertising rose at a rate of 40 per cent per year and in 1985 another barrier was broken. Lawyers began advertising for clients who would wish to sue specific named clients. When the Supreme Court approved that tactic, the deluge of lawsuits was underway.

Lawyers flooded the mailboxes of potential plaintiffs with advertising designed to solicit lawsuits to file. Whenever a major disaster happened,- ferryboat sinkings, airplane crashes, mine cave-ins, roof cave-ins - the lawyers immediately went to waiting areas where relatives waited for hopeful news of their loved ones.

When the Exxon Valdez went aground with so much oil spillage, The Wall Street Journal reported that "Liability lawyers and prostitutes fresh from nearby Anchorage, were prowling the dark, smoky bars in search of clients before the oil hit the beach. One woman, Sue Baird, a salmon fisherman, got calls from twenty lawyers within hours of the disaster.

The large law firms began using public relations representatives to stir up clients.

Without warning, a New York City urologist was hit by a law suit with all kinds of charges over complications that had supposedly developed during a prostrate surgery that he had performed. The charges were that the doctor was not properly trained, that he had negligently hired assistants without adequate training, and that he had developed complications that sometimes result in this type of surgery.

The lawyers had simply inserted every charge into the law suit that have ever been claimed for his type of surgery without there being any basis for that charge. The doctor had been trained at prominent universities, the training of his assistants had never been investigated and the indicated complications had never occurred in this particular patient.

Legal writers have developed handbooks for various types of liability claims. Lawyers have been known to copy a list of complaints from such a handbook word for word without ever investigating whether they apply to the case for which they are bringing a suit.

What seems to be happening is that some lawyers simply point a telescope in some direction at random and then decide on some kind of charges against the person or entity that falls within the range of vision. A reason can be found to sue everyone.

Lawyers don't only sue selected targets either with cause or at random. They also sue other lawyers for malpractice. The most common claim in such a suit is that some lawyer or corporation has been sued by a given lawyer. Then that lawyer gets sued for a large sum in turn because he omitted some charge that could have been included in the suit which he filed. That common practice causes the attorney who files a liability suit to include every charge that comes to mind to avoid being sued, that without investigating to see whether the added charge is valid or not.

The National Law Journal reported that in a two year period, nearly forty percent of law firms were sued. It also estimated that every law graduate who passes the bar today can expect to be sued for malpractice three times in his working career.

Similarly the class action suits are hammering at every potential target. If that lawyer seeks entry into the class of the wealthy, he need merely identify some improper conduct or something perceived as improper, and the suit can be filed which will put him into the ranks of millionaires. Often these may be nuisance suits with a sole goal to convince the target to decide to yield to the charges to save what may be honest costs of defending itself.

It takes little imagination to understand that if the number of liability suits have grown from a relative trickle in 1987 when the industry broke loose from all restraints into a mighty flood in 2002, and if all of that money transferred comes not from the doctors, the lawyers, or the corporations, but from the American people, what is it going to be like in 2017, particularly for those who are responsible enough to purchase the liability insurance? That is truly a crisis, possibly understood only by the people who carefully follow the trend of legal practice?

This developing crisis occurs slowly with so many victims, first in the rise of inflation, and indeed many of the poor do not understand what causes inflation. Inflation comes slowly but even the most uneducated understand that the prices are going up. Secondly, there is the loss of beneficial practices or products. We look at some examples.

The producers of various vaccines have been sued for every conceivable claim. The lawyers can always find some user of that vaccine who is willing to claim that he or she is suffering an ailment that is attributable to that vaccine. Many of the producers shut down their research that would have created some new vaccines that would have helped thousands or even millions of people.

Cars may have a $1000 higher sticker cost which relates directly to the many law suits against the manufacturers. Vast costs are added to many physical sites because of the necessity to cover "slip and fall" insurance.

These deprivations go unnoticed because how many people can know of what might have been available except for some of the lawsuits. A cure for Alzheimer's disease? If it might have been available, that fact may remain unknown because the company is afraid to introduce it because of fear of lawsuits? A cheap way to

215

provide desalinized water? Maybe the innovators feared that they could be held liable because trace amounts of truly harmless chemicals showed up in the product so the process was not introduced.

There can be no other condition in our future but a major crisis in the number of liability law suits. A rapid expansion of innovative methods to find new reasons to sue and new routes around every attempt to provide a bit of tempering reform can only mean a disaster rolling down the tracks toward us.

The catastrophic part of it all is that it is similar to the farming area along a large river that regularly suffers a spring flood. At some section of the river, it destroys the life sustaining plantings upon which the economy of the area depends. The floods can always find a new segment of the river to attack.

We had the swarm of lawsuits with their punitive action awards directed against the asbestos companies, tobacco companies, medical profession, automobile manufacturers, airplane manufacturers, corporate managers and corporations in general.

Unfortunately, creation of that list of targets is an unfinished symphony. As long as the economy survives, creative lawyers can repeatedly add a new industry. They need merely find some scientist who is willing to testify that the product or service causes potential health threats, environmental threats, or whatever impositions on our daily life, and then assemble a gullible jury that can be manipulated, and the forecasts of heavy rain begin.

One successful jury award in the millions of dollars and the river begins to overflow the bank. The next litigious lawyer can build on the work of the pioneer and soon thousands of lawyers can be hurling lawsuits against that industry. Then, it is on to the next selected industry.

A recent report suggested that lawyers are now thinking of ways to attack the glass industry. Imagine the impact if a scientist, maybe for financial rewards, declares that some component of glass is a potential cause of cancer. The manufacturers of every kind of glass could be sued. The building supply companies and construction firms could be sued. Then add every house builder who ever put glass windows in a home. The lawyers would vow to protect the public from the horrible threat to the American children.

The asbestos industry is the perfect example. Only 40 people develop mesothelonia each year, a miniscule number compared to 17,000 deaths from highway accidents each year, yet the lawyers are still destroying traces of the asbestos industry. We are supposed to forget the many benefits that are intrinsic to products of the asbestos industry.

■ ▪ ■ ▪ ■ ▪ ■ ▪ ■ ▪ ■ ▪ ■ ▪ ■ ▪ ■ ▪ ■

Exploding Number of Vicious Criminals at Large

A second certain crisis can be described which lies directly at the foot of the politicians. It is easy to blame them for inadequate funding for new jails and prisons but the problem goes much deeper than that. True, that is one part of a larger problem but they have also caused an overall problem by creating rules whereby the wrong criminals are sent to prison.

The great escalation of crime began with the activist Warren Supreme Court that coincided with the greatest deluge of births in American history. For forty years, the crime rate has climbed and will continue unless major changes are made in our justice system. Periods of reduced crime rates occur and the politicians boast that the decreasing number of arrests is because they have been tough on crime.

Any careful analyst, however, will conclude that the trend of crime comes in waves following in the path about 15 to 18 years behind the track line of the birth rate. The great wave of baby boomers were born in greatest numbers from 1945 to 1965 so the rate of crime soared as those children reached their highest crime years from 1960 to 1980. Birth rates declined from 1965 to 1985 as baby boomers became too old for child bearing. The ensuing reduced birth rate and not the action of the politicians led to a reduction of crimes from 1980 to 2000 as a reduced number of children grew into the heaviest crime years. The crime rate is ready to elevate again as children of the baby boomers enter into their highest crime years. Those entrants into the third wave of criminals show signs of being more violent and more incomprehensible than either of the two earlier waves. The number of vicious crimes is five times what it was 40 years ago.

Yet we are trying to stem the crime wave with essentially the same correctional system that we were using at that time. There has been only a minimal rise in the number of judges, courtrooms, support personnel, prisons and jails.

In addition, we can't keep the judges that we do have because a successful attorney in private practice can earn as much as 10 times more than a judge. The judges are leaving to take other more lucrative positions and yet hold on to their pensions.

The most crucial betrayal of the cause of justice in the past two decades has been the hypocritical adoption of "three strikes and you're out laws". That allows the politicians to use sound bites claiming to be tough on crime but those laws, along with the exclusionary rule from the Warren court, provide the breeding environment for the worst crime wave to date. And if those two problems aren't eliminated, may heaven help us.

Some "third strike laws" are worse than others because some have the saving salvation that the third of the three crimes has be a serious, violent crime. But other states, and here California is a leader as in so many venturesome efforts, have a law which states that even if the third strike is shoplifting, minor theft, small amount of drugs, or breaking and entering, the convicted person is sentenced to 40 years to life.

And what of the person who is charged with murder, bank robbery, child abuse resulting in death, kidnappings? Unless they are high profile cases, they will normally go through the plea bargain procedure because there aren't enough court rooms or judges to try them all. And not enough jails and prisons to hold them all if convicted. The jails and prisons are too full of those who committed shoplifting, use of a small amount of marijuana, forgeries, muggings, and infractions of political correctness.

What happens to the bank robbers and murderers? With an inadequate number of judges, court room support personnel, prosecuting personnel and prison facilities, the important crimes are plea bargained down to lesser offenses subject to short term sentences. Murderers agree to plead guilty to manslaughter with very reduced sentences. Bank robbers may get away with "Leaving the scene of a crime" and so may be sentenced to no more than the length of imprisonment already served. There just aren't the personnel or facilities to process the mass of criminals who are not subject to "third strike and you're out".

Judge Burton S. Katz, former Los Angeles judge has explored the problem in depth in his book, *Justice Overruled*, and has provided the following insight:

A thug encounters you on a dark street and mugs you. He has two strikes on his record so, after he heists your rings and wallet, he now faces a dilemma. Should he kill you, leave no witness, and face 25 years to life if he is convicted of your death? Or should he allow you to escape, leave a witness, and face 40 years to life if convicted"

The judge has provided a seven point program to overcome the great crime problems that now exist.

A. Provide a larger infrastructure for crime fighting – more police, more courtroom facilities, more judges, more public defenders, more prisons and more jails.

B. Guaranteed full time sentencing for first and second offenders who have committed a violent crime.

C. Amend the three strike laws to apply after three serious, violent crimes and eliminating the lesser crimes as reason for third strike long term commitment.

D. No early parole. You do the crime, you do the time.

E. Alternative sentencing for non-violent and non-serious crimes.

F. Juvenile criminals need to be incarcerated just like adults and be required to serve their full sentence, but to be sentenced to special prisons where they will be taught job skills and attain more education.

G. Prosecutorial Discretion should be provided where under special circumstances a judge or prosecution attorney may be justified in ignoring the six above guidelines.

In the above guidelines, serious or violent crimes would include burglaries in the night, robberies, kidnappings, deadly assaults, murders, rapes, and forcible child molestation. Although Judge Katz didn't mention these, I would add serious drug violations and drunken driving.

Chapter 28

The Critical Creeping Crisis

An examination of the apparently unsolvable crisis over constitutional protection demands strong knowledge of the earliest struggle for human rights. Let me clarify that while the information in this chapter is to be found in numerous texts and encyclopedia, it is best summed up in the book, "The Tyranny of Good Intentions" by Paul Craig Roberts and Lawrence M. Stratton and published by Prima Publishing.

The significant beginning occurred in the ninth century when Alfred the Great caused the laws of England to be codified as Hammurabi had done some 2700 years earlier. The Babylonian codes, however, had shown no serious concern for human rights. Many rights with which we are familiar showed up for the first time in Alfred's codes, sometimes in very crude forms.

The right to "ride to the king" would evolve into "due process". "A man's home is his castle" became the right not to have a home searched without a proper search warrant. "No taxation without representation" became a rallying cry in the development of revolutionary fervor in the thirteen colonies. "No man can be forced to testify against himself". Without this right, representatives of the sovereign could be very innovative in designing torture - torture racks, pulleys that would hoist the accused into the air by the wrists with weights attached to the feet, thumb screws, and creative methods for removing thumbnails or toenails.

Centuries later, the Magna Carta accomplished two things. When the nobles forced King John to sign the famous document at Runnymede in 1215, rights were established for the barons against the king. Not so widely publicized was that those rights had a corollary. The barons agreed to establish rights for the free men against themselves.

All Englishmen now had rights, maybe inconsistently enforced, but they were rights that came to be known as the "Rights of Englishmen". These protections were relatively effective until about 1600 when in the reigns of James I, Charles I, and James II, the sovereigns declared themselves to be holding kingships by divine right rather than by grant of power from the people. That, of course, meant that all "rights" could be ended at the whim of the kings. Parliament, as representative of the people, executed the first two kings and drove the third into exile.

Yet, the assaults on the "Rights of Englishmen" were not finished. Beginning in 1765, William Blackstone, college lecturer, authored *"Blackstone Commentaries on the Laws of England"* and they became the highly respected version of English law. Those volumes became the most famous documents ever written. Blackstone's work has since been criticized as poor law but they emphasized the law as a guarantor of liberty.

Then a strange thing happened. A new phenomena was taking place in the American colonies. The custom developed that every colonist who could read should know and understand the principles of the *"Blackstone Commentaries on the Rights of Englishmen."* Book publishing companies reported that as many copies of the Commentaries were being sold in the colonies with their small population of less than three million as were sold in all of England with its far greater population.

Indeed, the American Declaration of Independence, the Constitution and the Bill of Rights were written by men who had learned their law directly or indirectly from Blackstone's *Commentaries on the Law of England*. The basis of law as written and described by Blackstone was that the law was to serve as a shield.

Meanwhile, in England, a very different phenomenon was occurring. A very unusual young man, precocious to say the least, sat as a student in Blackstone's class at Oxford University. Jeremy Bentham was soon publishing anonymous tracts ridiculing the concepts of law shielding the accused against abuse. In his version, the law should be exercised to provide the greatest happiness for the greatest number of people. Bentham endorsed torture to persuade a guilty person to confess, the larger populace benefiting by getting the criminal off the streets. He called "liberty" a fictitious legal entity.

"The age we live in is a busy age; in which knowledge is rapidly advancing toward perfection".

He believed that social engineering to enhance the greater good took precedence over the Rights of Englishmen.

"Government is good in proportion to the happiness of which it is productive on the part of the body of people subject to it."

Jeremy Bentham believed in the wisdom and perfectibility of public administrators.

Richard Posner has commented on Bentham:

"In his suggestions for reform, Bentham was a pioneer in developing the technique known as brainwashing. He toyed with the idea of having everyone's name tattooed on his body to facilitate criminal law enforcement. Compulsory self-incrimination, torture, anonymous informers, abolition of the attorney-client privilege and of the jury, and depreciation of rights are other parts of Bentham's legacy to totalitarian regimes."

Bentham's ideas spread throughout England with the result that, by the time of the American Revolution, the Americans were stronger believers in the Rights of Englishmen than were the English.

When he died in 1832, Jeremy Bentham was surrounded by 70,000 pages of unpublished manuscripts. A century after his death, the ideas propounded by Bentham were to surface in a form more iniquitous than even he had considered.

Following Bentham and his plan of make the greatest number happy, the German Reichstag on March 23, 1933 passed the Enabling Act granting the German cabinet the authority to establish any law by executive edict. The world would call the new order Nazism. Soon, Adolph Hitler would utilize Bentham's doctrine of providing the greatest happiness for the greatest number to justify purifying the Nordic race, a euphemism for eliminating Jews. It was Benthanism at its worst.

Article I of the U.S. Constitution states very unequivocally that all legislative power shall be vested in a Congress of the United States. The battle for the Executive Department to take over the law making powers started early in the history of the new nation. From *The Tyranny of Good Intentions*

"The requirement in Article I that Congress shall make all laws has been ignored for the greatest part of the twentieth century...The most powerful legislators, those who construct the decrees that most directly impact people's lives are entrenched in the federal bureaucracy."

The gradual beginnings of Benthanism in the United States were described in *"New Commentaries on the Criminal Law"* by 19th century writer Joel Prentiss Bishop. Then, in the twentieth century, the chopping process was to remove a giant chip from the Rights of Englishmen. A 1922 Supreme Court decision, called by a Stanford professor "adjudication at its worst", ruled that "intent was not required to constitute a crime". A plea of good faith or ignorance was no longer sufficient. This was removal of one of the strongest shields that had come from Blackstone.

As a major outpost of defense of the constitution, former Supreme Court Justice John Marshall Stone wrote in 1892,

"That congress cannot delegate legislative power to the president is a principle universally recognized as vital to the integrity and maintenance of the system of government ordained by the Constitution."

Although the constitution authorizes 57 separate powers or responsibilities for one or both houses of congress, no where does it grant the power to delegate it's duty of making laws.

The decade of the 1930s was a pivotal one for the surrender of legislative powers to the executive branch all around the world. In Russia, Joseph Stalin took over total power as an absolute dictator. In Italy, Benito Mussolini became the sole ruler of Italy with only a figurehead legislature. In Nazi Germany, the German Reichstag delegated all powers to Adolph Hitler.

The principle of congress not having power to delegate was not to survive in the United States. In 1933, a horde of influential lawyers rode into Washington openly working to transfer law-making power from the legislature to the executive branch of government. James M. Landis and Felix Frankfurter, future Supreme Court Justice, were leaders of the pack.

The New Deal was a spring board from which the use of regulations issued by one agency or another would expand it's own power using as it's authority such terms as "promoting the public interest", "fair and equitable prices," "fighting against excessive profits", or "imminent hazards of public safety".

The people were so concerned about the problems caused by the depression that they expressed no objection when the multiple agencies of the New Deal were given widespread powers which should not have been delegated by Congress.

Thereafter, when the nation faced a crisis, be it the depression of the thirties, the civil rights struggle of the fifties, the battle against drugs in the eighties, or the war against terror in the 21st century, a principal weapon was to create laws, not in congress, but in the labyrinth of bureaucracy. Those laws, of course, were known as regulations but they often took on the full impact of laws.

In 1933, the Germans made the transfer of power to executive edicts with a single legislative act and we called it Nazism. In the United States, we have passed law after law which have cancelled protections provided by the constitution and then added executive edicts at an astounding rate. The Federal Register which updates federal regulations daily totaled 80,332 pages of bureaucratic regulations in the single year of 2002.

We are supposed to believe, as did Bentham, that these are fully authorized laws and regulations which benefit the greatest number.

We must examine a few specific examples of trampling on the protections guaranteed by the constitution. These are but representative of thousands of violations that occur daily.

Possibly, the most flagrant and most often used violation has been the Comprehensive Forfeiture Act of 1984.

The statute states that "The following shall be subject to forfeiture to the United States and no property right shall exist in them." The following paragraphs list the personal properties that can be confiscated on presumption alone. The list includes: "aircraft, vehicles, vessels, moneys, negotiable instruments, securities, firearms, raw materials, products or equipment, controlled substances, paraphernalia, plus books, records and research." On real property, the following were declared forfeitable: "all real property, including any rights, title or interest in the whole of any lot or tract of land and any appurtenances or improvements if such is used, or intended to be used, in any manner or part, to commit, or to facilitate the commission of a violation of this subchapter".

The presumptive seizure of property permitted by the act inflicts punishment without proof. It reverses the presumption of innocence. This act clearly authorizes violations of the constitution.

It has had far reaching impacts. The Act was intended to give drug law enforcers the tools that it needed to fight drug trafficking. We can hope that the police do not choose to use it beyond where they have genuine cause to believe that violations are occurring.

However, it has happened often enough to be greatly alarmed about the openings it gives to circumvent the constitution. In October, 1992, thirty armed police officers broke down the door of the home on the 200 acre estate of multimillionaire Donald Scott and shot him dead. He had committed no crime, and had defied no summons.

Mr. Scott's oceanfront property, with scenic vistas, was surrounded on three sides by a federal park. Park officials had been trying to add his property to the park, but he had refused to sell. Mr. Scott's murder was termed "self defense". The confiscation was justified by a claim that he had 3000 marijuana plants growing on his property. A subsequent search of the property found no marijuana plants.

The worst of the provisions for confiscation is the one that allows any amount of cash over $100 to be considered to be drug money and so, subject to seizure. Fortunately, no episode has been publicized where a representative of government has exercised that power except where the amount of cash is great. In one case, however, Selma Washington had $19,000 that represented a home insurance settlement from hurricane damage and was on her way to purchase repair materials when a police officer seized the money on the presumption that it was drug money. An attorney was able to recover about 80% of it.

This property seizure provision almost became personal. After my father passed away in 1979, my mother was independent enough to travel to most areas of the United States and Europe. The one area that she had never visited was the deep South of our own country. My wife, ever anxious to please her mother-in-law, decided to remedy that. She persuaded me that we should take her on a trip in our motor home. We visited Houston, the French Quarter of New Orleans, the Bellingrath Gardens of Mobile and went down into Florida as far as Ocala. Then we returned home through St Augustine, Savannah, Charleston and Ashville. Finally, we were driving westward across Arkansas when the state police thought they had themselves a motor home.

I was driving and my 85 year old mother was riding "shotgun" when I saw the flashing red light of a state trooper. I had been traveling well below the speed limit and had neither passed anyone nor made an improper turn. What was wrong?

The bubble popped for the patrolman when my wife appeared near my shoulder at the same time that he reached the door and asked for my driver's license. The trooper asked if he could go through our motor home. I had no reason not to allow it and, after he had completed a brief search, he went back to his patrol car to talk to authorities by radio. Eventually, he returned and told me we could proceed.

I informed him that since he had invaded the sanctity of my home, he should explain what was happening. After stalling a bit, he explained that a motor home with Colorado license plates and two elderly persons aboard had left Florida with a load of drugs and was headed for our home state. With my graying hair, I seemed to be the second half of the elderly couple that was supposedly unaware of the illegal cargo that they were hauling. Yet, the reports hadn't indicated a third person on board.

If they had found even a single ounce of marijuana, they had a full right to confiscate our motor home. In just such an occurrence, a pair of young newlyweds who were acquaintances of a friend of mine in Seattle borrowed a car to make a short honeymoon trip into Canada. On the return across the border, the car was searched and a single marijuana cigarette was found, apparently left by some former occupant. The car was confiscated and the young couple was left without transportation back to Seattle. In a suburb of that city, it has been announced that when drugs are discovered in any rental property, the property will be confiscated without recourse for the owner.

Is this the kind of protection we were given by the Bill of Rights? Case after case has occurred where the police or drug agents have seized valuable property under the guise of complying with the act. Constitutional rights are being dismantled.

It is to be emphasized that the forfeiture act is only one of many that authorize clear violations of the protected rights given us under the constitution.

Let's mention one more clause of the constitution that has been overridden. Article I Section 9 of the constitution clearly states that there shall be no ex post facto laws, such laws being adopted after the crime has been committed. Yet, as the last act during the administration of Jimmy Carter, Congress passed the Comprehensive Environmental Response, Compensation and Liability Act. The act created what was to be known as the Superfund and provided for the conviction of violators who had committed the offense long before the law prohibiting it was passed.

A principle has been firmly established that if a great wave of public support can be generated with the help of the news media, then any protection of the constitution is subject to being eliminated in practice. What if in some future generation, there is widespread support for eliminating Jews? Or persons of Norwegian descent? (That would include this author.)

We face a dilemma of awesome proportion. We have great threats to the health and welfare of the people of the United States. That can mean drugs, terror attacks or war. Some of our most revered leaders have demanded bold initiatives to overcome those problems and in the wake of the leadership of such men as Franklin Roosevelt, John Kennedy, Ronald Reagan or George W. Bush, the legislature has adopted laws that override the Bill of Rights. We probably can't go back to full protection from that constitution adopted in 1787.

Clearly, I have no workable solution to these worsening trends. Have I mentioned that lawyers have been involved in originating every one of the laws, rules and regulation that wiped out the protections?

Chapter 29

Lawyers to be of Good Character?

We would expect that admittance to the bar would be limited to men and women of good character. Surely, we can assume that at the top levels of our court systems, the federal and state supreme courts are committed to limiting admission to practice of law to those who have established sound character. Can we really truly assume that?

Let's see what light Justice Kane, Jr. of the U.S. District Court of Colorado had to offer:

"Should an applicant for admission to the bar be admitted when it is shown, without contest, that he killed another while driving under the influence, declared bankruptcy to escape the $200,000 civil judgment, perjured himself in a deposition taken in aid of execution of the judgment, filed a false application for admission by stating he had paid almost $7000 on the judgment when he had in fact made no such voluntary payments at all even though he had an income of $90,000 per year and a home equity of $225,000? If your answer is yes, go to the head of the class. - - - at least in Florida where the state's Supreme Court said, 'We recognize that (he) may have continuing moral obligations to the family of the man he negligently killed, but to permit such considerations in a petition for admission to the bar would require the making of such <u>SUBTLE DISTINCTIONS</u> that no satisfactory rule could <u>be devised</u>.' Of his admitted perjury and concealment of assets, the court said not one word.

"Should an attorney be disbarred who admits to having a felony conviction for delivering cocaine to a minor, for possessing cocaine and who admits to having injecting a nineteen year old girl with cocaine, and taking a fifteen year old girl to a toilet in a drugstore where he injects her and himself with cocaine? Right again. The Supreme Court of Florida says a three year old <u>nunc pro tunc</u> suspension is enough because the never disbarred attorney has demonstrated positive efforts to rid himself of the (drug) dependency."

"Should the first United States District Judge to be convicted on a bill of impeachment by the United States Senate be disbarred from practicing law after serving 17 months in (prison)? Not according to the Supreme Court of Nevada.

"Should an applicant be denied admission who improperly passed himself off as a police officer, made material misstatements about prior addresses and place of employment in his character and fitness application? Well, this question has a trick answer to it by the Supreme Court of Illinois. In its wisdom, that Court said the applicant could not be admitted on the basis of the false application but he could gain admission forthwith by filing a new application.

In Colorado, these pressing questions are more difficult to answer. For example an attorney who engaged in fraud, deceit, and misrepresentation prejudicial to the administration of justice and who was found to have given testimony in the grievance proceeding which was not credible was not disbarred. A one year suspension was considered adequate.

"On the other hand, a lawyer who abandoned his meager practice and left the state without a forwarding address with the Clerk of the Supreme Court was disbarred. But a lawyer who wrote himself into the final will of a client whose testamentary capacity was questionable thereby depriving a charity of a significant bequest and then served as personal representative for the estate was not disbarred. A lawyer who wrote checks for insufficient funds was disbarred but a lawyer who forged a will was not."

Logically, there are some people who are quitting the practice of law because of conscience and it is happening more and more. In one 1984 poll by the American Bar Association Journal, 41 percent of lawyers said they would rather be doing something else but most of those complained of endless hours of meaningless work. An estimated 40,000 lawyers are leaving the profession each year. Those who do withdraw for reasons of convenience reinforce the need for a reconstruction of law practice and court procedure.

Sam Benson quit after two years of law and wrote in an op-ed column of Newsweek,

"I was tired of the deceit. I was tired of the chicanery. But most of all, I was tired of the misery my job caused other people."

Chief of Police Lester Langford of Cherry Hills, Colorado summed up the situation this way,

"The court system is like an old engine that is all fouled up with years and years of sludge. What we are doing is to repeatedly put in additives to try to solve the problems when the real problem is that there is sludge in every part of the engine."

The chief also believes that the trial of O.J. Simpson for murdering his wife Nicole and her friend Ronald Coleman may have been one of the best things that ever happened in the history of American jurisprudence because it allowed the average American to observe the judicial process closely.

"The public saw the deceptions, the finagling, the circus atmosphere that the two sides put on to try to promote their cases...We saw this case day in and day out, the lawyers looking for loopholes, looking for technicalities, looking into the background of the officers who made the case, trying to dredge up as much junk to throw into the air to hopefully persuade one juror at a time that 'yeah, that's right' whether the accused is guilty or innocent. We've got to do something to speed up the process and cut down the loopholes and get a better product out of this."

That benefit was particularly effective since there appeared to be an insurmountable amount of evidence indicating that Simpson was guilty and yet he was found innocent. That education of the American public was the first step toward correcting the abuses of the system, the first hope of removing the sludge out of the system.

An earlier title for this book used the word "obdurate" to describe the practice of law. That word is so totally indicative of the problems of the legal profession that I shall define it for those few who did not know the meaning of the word and were not inclined to resort to the dictionary.

The word "obdurate" is an adjective meaning that one's own sense has been so deadened to the evil tendencies within one's own self that he or she or it no longer recognizes the evil that is committed. Conscience can no longer function. That definition is true of the overall profession of law and most of the individuals who practice within its realm.

Could the George Flatter trials in Detroit be labeled as show case trials where a confession and three consecutive convictions were thrown out on technicalities before a fifth jury finally declared the man innocent in a 1966 trial? By the time of that final trial, several of the witnesses had died.

The reader could easily reach the impression that I am in favor of eliminating the lawyer's involvement in the judicial system or of stopping the practice of law.

That obviously cannot be done. The lawyers are indispensable in bringing order out of the chaos that they have created and that would otherwise exist among the rules, procedures and regulations that hold the organizations of our society, particularly government, together.

What we can do is to do our best to blunt the swords which are the essence of the adversarial system and the bureaucratic nightmare.

Justice Kane has stated that,

> "The legal procedures we use are simply no longer capable of fulfilling the purpose for which they were conceived... Many of the complaints about lawyer competence are rooted in the impossibility of anyone being able to cope with inadequacies of the system."

Overall goals for improvement should be fivefold:

- ✓ To maintain and restore all of the rights that were instituted in the Bill of Rights as adopted in 1791.
- ✓ To achieve a state such that when a criminal trial is conducted, the procedures are dedicated to determining truth, honesty and fairness and not be a system that serves the lawyers.
- ✓ To achieve a state where the legal system utilizes the best resources that are available.
- ✓ To achieve a state where a finding of innocent corresponds with not having committed the crime and does not mean having achieved a victory under the rules of the lawyers.
- ✓ To dismantle the power structure which principally serves the legal profession with wealth, access to power, and control over the lives of most Americans.

It may seem to the reader that I have gone to excess to point out so many of the perceived flaws that have been generated in the legal process. It was important, however that I make a strong case that the system is so intrinsically flawed, so in need of repair, that drastic measures have to be taken. Halfway measures are not enough.

Chapter 30

What is Good About the Legal Profession?

Over 25 chapters have been presented that have skewered the legal profession. Now it is time to dedicate a single chapter to acknowledging the positive contributions which that profession has made to our American way of life.

The legal profession has provided one of the great gifts to humanity, namely, the privilege for 50,000 people each year, mostly at a youthful age, to make career decisions to practice law with an understanding that it provides the satisfaction of doing good, of helping those who need help. Unfortunately, the practice of law has not lived up to its promise.

The role of the lawyers has been to give form to civilization. The earliest patterns of civilizations were created by the hunters and gatherers, and then the herders and growers functioned still without significant need for lawyers. As soon as commerce and governments began to develop, however, lawyers were required to provide the procedural forms by which civilization would continue to advance for the next four thousand years.

The documents needed to build governments and the definition of relationships in civil systems has mostly been done by lawyers. The laws have been written and treaties negotiated by lawyers.

Lawyers are the ones who are there with the responsibilities for protecting the freedoms that were given to us by the Constitution and the Bill of Rights. Although adherence to those responsibilities is selective, they still provide certain protections. Without lawyers, prisoners would languish in our jails and prisons far beyond reasonable requirements.

Those who are charged with crimes are defended by lawyers, whether too zealously or with inadequate representation is not a matter of consistency.

Marriage was given to us by the church and the various forms of religion. Divorce and nuptial agreements were created by lawyers.

Lawyers invented the forms for corporations, trusts, wills, bond issues, receiverships, acquisitions, mergers, etc. All are beneficial; yet, they chiefly serve the wealthy and the near wealthy.

I have written that I worked 8 years essentially as a contract lawyer, but I can not take credit for creative work, because it has been the lawyers who have developed the meanings of the various conditions and terms that constitute the backbone of every contract.

All of those accomplishments certainly make law stand high among the outstanding professions.

Books and movie scripts are abundant which portray the good, even heroic, deeds performed by defense attorneys. Every time that a defense attorney wins a front page case, the attorneys and the reporters proclaim the triumph of justice.

In the real world, however, those great feats of defense attorneys rescuing an accused from the jaws of injustice and freeing the innocent are harder to identify with a sure vision. Yet the profession does occasionally offer opportunity for a heroic effort that is to be applauded, possibly more than any other undertaking.

Maybe no more noble and heroic undertaking ever occurred than the defense effort in behalf of "The Dummy" who was twice charged with murdering prostitutes in the slum area of Chicago in 1965 and 1972. The story is related in the book *"Dummy"* written by Earnest Tidyman and published by Little Brown and Company in 1976.

Danny Lang was a deaf mute with his handicap caused by a severe childhood disease. The death of both prostitutes occurred after servicing Danny, age 19 at the time of the first death, as a customer. Those were suspicious circumstances but police were unable to question Danny in a way that his responses had clear meaning. His hand signals could ambiguously be interpreted as having multiple meanings.

Attorney Lowell Mason, himself a deaf person, waged one of the great battles in legal history. Authorities were quite willing to imprison Danny Long without a trial or to send him to a center for the criminally insane but the one thing that they could not do was to conduct a trial with Lang being given his proper legal rights. The state of Illinois simply had a case for which there was no logical and legal path to trial; yet they would gladly argue to put him away. Those rights were violated time after time with Lowell having to fight the battles.

In the case of the second murder, Danny was finally sentenced to a prison term in spite of evidence that had a high probability of indicating his innocence. Yet it is the potential for such a great effort by an attorney under the most difficult of circumstances with which we are concerned. Unless we are talking about a doctor's life and death struggle to save a person's life, no occupation could have provided a greater call for noble effort.

Chapter 31

To a Better Justice System!

Former Judge John L. Kane, Jr., whom I have quoted often in this book, wrote:

> "The U.S. criminal justice system is seen as excessively expensive, conceptually confused, increasingly unfair, and pervasively ineffectual".

Lawyers will proclaim, maybe unanimously, that any existing problems in the American legal system are theirs to correct. And so it should be if they had a history of creating systems and procedures that function well. They still have the power to do it if they can gather the determination to correct the glitches and remove the rock piles.

What should be considered the most critical improvements to be made? On a larger scale, that should be elimination of the adversarial system, but that is going to come hard. That system serves the personal interests of the lawyers too well.

As a major part of that improvement, however, the exclusionary rule should be eradicated entirely and the barriers to acceptance of confessions should be minimized. In spite of the widespread claims, these actions would not mean infringement on rights granted under the constitution. They would be infringement against rights posted by man-made rules.

Confessions should be denied into evidence only if an amount of compulsion was used that would be an affront to the conscience of a reasonable person in regard to physical torture, threats of violence, denial of sleep, denial of food, relay questioning, or intimidation. Even some of those should require proof of being excessive.

The greatest urgency to improve the legal status for the most people, however, would be to loosen the shackles on paralegals to allow them to serve those persons who are unable to afford lawyers. Pro bono work is dreadfully insufficient.

Assuredly, paralegals would make mistakes but the problems caused by their assistance would be far less damaging than for them to do without legal help. Let there be no more Montes who labor for 13 months and never receive a penny of pay for their work because they can't afford a lawyer.

Finally, there is the improvement that is beyond any reasonable horizon and that is the restoration of rights supposedly provided by the Bill of Rights. In extreme circumstances, those infringements are temporarily justified in such situations as war, terror attacks, and the drug trade but the violations have spread far beyond reason to every segment of American life. They should be removed when the crisis is past.

My sole fear in writing this book is that it may tend to disillusion some young lawyers and potential lawyers who are either making their way through law school or are in the beginning years of practice.

According to Tillinghast-Towers Perrin, an insurance consulting firm, liability lawsuits in 1950 took a half percent of the gross domestic product of our nation. That has risen so that today, those lawsuits claim a five times higher share of GDP. That is a very steep rate of climb.

Let's summarize into a single paragraph, the practices of the legal profession. The higher courts - the United States Supreme Court, the eleven U.S. Courts of Appeal, and the state supreme courts have attempted to convert all applicable laws and the constitution into a set of possibly 100,000 rules. Maybe it would be a million. The rules are contradictory and ill defined. No attorney or judge can know them all. A trial judge sometimes has to guess which rules will be applied on the next appellate decision. Often political considerations determine which rules will be selected and how they will be combined into a decision. The personal beliefs of some judge or combination of judges enter into decisions. Defense attorneys search the endless ambiguous rules until they find some on which they can base an appeal. Then the public screams about convictions being overturned on technicalities.

Individual lawyers may not believe in falsifications of the trial but they behave as though they do; or they at least tolerate the falsifications in silence. Each member of the legal profession who capitulates to "ideological pseudo-veracity" becomes a petty instrument of the lawyer's cult. This leads to an unprofessional lawyer with lowered morals upon whom the system depends. They become complicit in the pernicious conduct of falsification – the rejected evidence that could have pointed to the truth, the perjured testimony, and the discredited witness who was in fact totally truthful.

Every attempt has been made in this book to avoid political bias and to make references in that area only where examples provide particularly appropriate illustrations. The matter of achieving a justice system that provides fairer and more accurate decisions should not be a political issue unless supporters of lottery justice make it so by their political contributions.

In a clear statement for all of the world to read, let it be written that there is evil at work in our country consisting of the wrongful practice of law.

When an individual is admitted to the bar in spite of having been convicted of distributing cocaine to minors, or having injected cocaine into a 15-year-old girl, or who had fraudulently written himself into a will of a person who lacked testamentary capacity, those are all evidence of evil.

There is evil when a person bears false witness against his neighbor.

When lawsuits become so ever present that they deprive a segment of the American populace of the medical care that is essential to their well being, that is a matter of serious evil.

There is evil when a killer is freed because his lawyer uses fictitious testimony to convince or confuse the jury.

There is clearly evil when doctors are forced into a decision that it is better to let a patient die than to attempt a heroic life saving effort.

And we know there is evil if the lawyer charges his client for hours not worked.

If these are but isolated acts of evil, we know that the proliferation of acts of evil are as numerous as the vehicles on the streets and highways of America.

The American acceptance of the conduct of trial lawyers should make clear something that has disturbed people for over six decades. How could the great mass of German people have tolerated the evils of the Nazi regime when they had to have known at least in part what was going on? Now we deal with a lesser magnitude of evil but one in which most Americans know full well what is happening. Yet, we do nothing. We go on pretending that the criminal justice system is the realm of the lawyers and therefore that what they do is not the concern of the greater American populace whose members are fully occupied with their own concerns. The German people permitted themselves to believe that the death camps and the torture chambers were the realm of the Storm Troopers and therefore that what that group did was not the concern of the greater German populace. They, likewise, had been fully occupied with their own concerns.

While I have described numerous reforms, I am not anticipating that lawyers will promptly fall into line. However, I believe that most of the American people are honest and forthright and if they steadily press the objective of a better justice system, the American Bar will begin to accept the changes.

As I have informed people of the book that I have been preparing, I have almost always received an instant response that "I hate lawyers." With the reservoir of maybe fifty million lay people who are quick to respond with that statement, I believe it is logical to establish a great wave of discourse on changes that could be pressured on the legal profession. If enough people show a strong support, there will be politicians who will respond to the "will of the people". If enough people want it, some congressman or congresswoman will introduce legislation to establish the first tentative reforms. When those first reforms are used over time, they will win support for more and stronger reforms.

I have been asked if there is any action which we as individuals can take in the battle for a fairer and more accurate justice system. I do not know what course others may take but I know that for myself I will change my stand in regard to voting by "litmus test". I have always opposed those who have used the stand for or against abortion as a "litmus test'.

This time, however, I will be inquiring which candidates for high office are receiving the largest political contributions from the American Trial Lawyers Association. As my first ever votes by "litmus test", I will cast my ballot for the opponent of the recipient who receives large support from the American Trial Lawyers Association.

The lawyers defy demands for reform because they know they can get away with it. The more reforms that are placed into usage, the easier it will be to get the next one to follow. The people will be emboldened to stand up to the "entrenched nobility", and take this nation back from the swarms of lawyers. We must seize the moment.

Eventually, the legal profession will be inspired to establish more critical reforms within their own system. At some point a much-improved "Procedures for Criminal Court Justice" will be adopted. The lawyers would prefer to have the terminology be in their own words to the greatest extent possible. Still, they will inevitably attempt to continue usage of the old procedures in defiance of new rules that may be promulgated.

We, the non-lawyering public, must maintain a tenacious sense of commitment.

Epilogue

The Study of Problems in the Legal Profession is a Bottomless Pit

This book was destined to be less than satisfactory to any author whether it be me or some person more learned in the law. The malpractice and evil that resides in the legal profession is a bottomless pit. The law is such a vast subject with so many aspects that it would take many years to fully explore the problems in the law and the legal profession.

Yet, a book to arouse the public to a need for reformation has been sorely needed. Events in our time are moving so rapidly that problems develop more swiftly than a single individual can keep up with them. The public needs to be better informed so as to become a force to require reformation. Without a true revolution, all will be lost. Unless the adversarial system of trial justice is replaced, the problems will forever be unsolved.

When I began a previous book, *Real Solutions to Real Problems*, I included 12 chapters discussing the problems in the legal profession as I saw them. In my only try at submitting that book to an agent, who incidentally was a lawyer, I received the appraisal that, "Mr. Sampson simply does not understand the discipline of lawyers". Hmmm!

Age cannot be denied. I am 82 years old at the time this book is published and even if I had the will to dedicate the remaining years of my contributable life, my eyes have paid the price and are unable to withstand the burden of additional reading. As source material for this book, I have read at least 30 books in search of truth about the profession of law. At least two dozen of those have been after reaching the age of 80.

I am certain that a genuine pursuit of a full understanding would travel through another 10 books, a couple dozen live interviews and maybe study of 20 new case histories. By then, my store of information would be out of date.

In addition, I would plan to increase my knowledge and understanding of the struggles of Alfred, the Great, in the ninth century, to the epic clash with King John which led to the Magna Carta at Runnymede, and to the battle against King James I, King Charles I, and King James II that ended only when these men were either executed or sent into exile. One needs to be knowledgeable on all of these struggles in order to fully understand the flawed practice of today.

If I can assist the suffering public in the struggle for a better system of law, I will always be available as long as my mental and physical facilities sustain me.

Yet, I must write. My next publishing venture is planned as a biography which will tentatively be entitled "Mary, the Indomitable One". That book will describe a woman who is not an egomaniacal exploiter of the headlines. Instead, half Black and half Cherokee, she is the essence of the human spirit. If I can properly describe her and her struggles, she should be established as a role model of what can be accomplished without a day of formal schooling, wealth or publicity agents. The book will be based mostly on personal interviews and thus will relieve me of the burden of extensive reading.

Selected Bibliography

Abramson, Jeffrey. *We, the Jury*, Cambridge: Harper-Collins 1994

Adler, Stephen J. *The Jury - Disorder in the Courts*, New York: Doubleday, 1955

Burnett, D. Graham. *A Trial by Jury*, New York: Alfred A. Knopf, 2001

Crier, Catherine, *The Case against Lawyers*, New York: Broadway Books, Division of Random House 2002

Grano, Joseph A. *Confessions, Truth and the Law*, Ann Arbor, MI: University of Michigan Press, 1993

Grisham, John, *The Firm*, et. al., New York: Doubleday, Misc

Hentoff, Nat, *Free Speech for Me but Not for Thee*, New York: Harper Collins, 1992

Hogrogian, John. *Miranda v. Arizona*, San Diego: Lucent Books, 1999

Howard, Philip. *The Death of Common Sense*, New York: Random House, 1994

Kane, John L, Jr. *Lectures at Denver University School of Law*, Denver, 1990

Katz, Burton S. *Justice Overruled*, New York: Warner Books, 1997

Linowitz, Saul M., *The Betrayal Profession*, New York: Charles Scribner & Sons, 1994

Olsen, Walter K, *The Litigation Explosion - What happened when they Unleashed the Lawsuit*, New York: Penguin Books, 1991

Olson, Walter K, *The Rule of Lawyers – How the New Litigation Elite Threatens America's Rule of Law*, New York: St. Martins Press, 2001

Petrocelli, Daniel, *Triumph of Justice – The Final Judgment of the Simpson Saga*, New York: Crown Publishers, 1998

Rhode, Deborah L., *In the Interests of Justice, Reforming the Legal Profession*, New York: Oxford University Press, 2000

Roberts, Paul Craig and Stratton, Lawrence M. *The Tyranny of Good Intentions*, Roseville, CA: Prima Publishing, Forum, 2000

Rothwax, Harold J. *Guilty: the Collapse of Criminal Justice.* New York: Random House, 1996

Schlesinger, Arthur, *The Disuniting of America*, New York: Norton Press, 1991

Spence, Gary. *O.J.-The Last Word*, New York: St. Martin's Press, 1997

About the Author

After graduating from the U.S. Naval Academy, Sampson anticipated a Naval career, but to avoid extensive separation from family, he made tough decisions to switch through a graduate degree in industrial management.

During 35 years of engineering and management, Al studied aspects of law at two universities. Through work experience, he gained considerable background in law and supplemented that by reading over 25 books by lawyers who have urged revolutionary changes in the practice of law.

By writing this book after his 80th birthday, he has fulfilled a lifelong dream of making a possible major contribution toward curing one of the ills of society.

With this book, the goal is to enroll the American public in the push for reform. The profession of law must serve all Amerians.

www.ingramcontent.com/pod-product-compliance
Lightning Source LLC
Chambersburg PA
CBHW030257290526
45785CB00001B/128